The 50-Day Shift

The 50-Day Shift

A Path to Personal Mastery

Zachary Fulbright

Thought by thought. Day by day. A better life.

For permissions or inquiries, please contact:
www.zacharyfulbright.com

First Edition
Printed in the United States of America

ISBN: 979-8-9988606-0-7
Cover design by The Book Designers

Interior design by Zachary Fulbright
Typeset in Georgia

Contents

To my sweet daughters, F. & F.

Live the example.

Be the end result you seek.

And only look for what you truly wish to find.

May your wings carry you precisely as far as you dream to travel.

Love always,

Daddy

...And to my Mother:

This is the book I was telling you about.

Introduction

Life is a journey—one full of highs, lows, and all the moments in between. Like many, I've often found myself torn between living up to others' expectations and staying true to my own path. The uncertainty of not knowing which direction to take can feel overwhelming. I've walked that tightrope, and it's exhausting. But we all have an inner compass—that quiet, powerful voice within—that helps guide us toward our true path. When we learn to tune in and listen, we stop battling between who we *should* be and who we *could* be, because we finally know who we *are*. This knowing—the realization that we each have the power to shape our lives and become who we're meant to be—is often called Self Mastery. But I prefer *Personal Mastery*, because that's what it is—*personal*. It's your story. It's the biography of your life, and *you alone are the author*. You're writing it, every step of the way.

My journey to personal-mastery began when I fully understood that I was the architect of my own life—that I had the power to shape my reality through my thoughts, emotions, and actions, and with it, the ability to create happiness, peace, and a sense of calm. That realization changed everything. It marked a turning point that led me to create this 50-day guide, designed to help you confidently choose the experiences that matter most—purpose, fulfillment, and joy—instead of just reacting to whatever life throws your way.

Throughout this journey, you'll discover simple tools and insights to help you take control and design the life you truly desire. Each day offers an opportunity for growth, and with consistent, small actions, you'll experience a powerful transformation, evolving into a new version of yourself with greater clarity, joy, and purpose.

The path ahead isn't about pushing yourself through constant struggle. It's about building healthy habits—whether it's taking a daily moment for yourself or nurturing a hobby you love. While each step might feel small, over time, those small actions add up to profound change. The beauty of this process lies in its simplicity and the power of consistency.

Throughout my life—as teacher, entrepreneur, father—I've come to realize that *true fulfillment comes from embracing deeper meaning in our lives and helping others along the way.* A few years ago, I reached a breaking point—burnt out from a career that had consumed me, my health rapidly declining, and overwhelmed by personal losses that felt too heavy to carry. I suddenly found myself alone, a single father —stuck, uncertain, and unsure how to move forward.

Then, everything changed. I paused, slowed down, and began reconnecting with who I truly was. Through deep introspection and a renewed commitment to myself, I rediscovered my purpose—and slowly began the long journey home. That time of solitude, healing, and self-reflection gave birth to this book—the culmination of everything I learned about resilience, growth, and transformation.

Whether you're feeling uncertain or seeking answers and meaning, this guide will help. Its principles will carry you through any challenge—empowering you to unlock your potential, one day at a time.

Personal mastery begins quietly—with small, approachable shifts that help you return to yourself. Then, like wading into the ocean, the shallow waters deepen, and each lesson grows more powerful. Change doesn't have to be overwhelming—it's about small, consistent steps forward. We all face struggles, and yes, life is hard at times. But as you walk this path, I promise you—you're not alone. The strength to move forward is already within you. You're about to take the first step in a transformative process—and this book will be your guide.

Let's begin. Your journey starts now.

You're more ready than you think.

Day 1.

Eliminate Limiting Beliefs

"We can do anything we choose if we eliminate limiting beliefs."

Everything begins with a goal—we visualize the desired outcome, and then plan the steps to achieve it. To become a gold medalist, we start by learning a sport and then work to master it. If being a teacher is our goal, our journey begins in school, where we earn a degree, pass the necessary exams, and then secure a job.

But how often do we choose not to pursue something because we talk ourselves out of it? We tell ourselves we're too old, too tired, don't have enough money, or just don't have the time. If we didn't have these thoughts, would anything stop us from being or becoming whatever or whoever we wanted to be?

If we couldn't find a reason not to do something, what would hold us back? These thoughts that keep us in our current state—the state that feels familiar—are limiting beliefs. A limiting belief is something we tell ourselves that restricts what we do. They're the "I'm too this" or "too that" beliefs—too old, too tired, too broke. But the truth is, a belief is simply something we repeat to ourselves over and over again. And we can do anything we choose if we eliminate our limiting beliefs.

Imagine life as a running path along a beach. The path stretches down the shore, past the beachgoers, until the last of them fades from view. Then, the trail continues through and beyond the sand dunes. If someone tells you, "Don't run past the dunes," how far will you go? Probably just to the dunes—because that's where you were told to stop.

If someone says, "Stop at the end of the dunes," you'll run to the end and stop. You see? This is how limiting beliefs affect our decisions.

If you ask how far you can run and are told, "As far as you want" or "As far as you can," how far will you go? You likely won't know the answer until you start running. This is what it's like to live without limiting beliefs—simply running, watching the progress, as the world unfolds around you.

And imagine what that feels like: the wind at your back, no one stopping you, no voice telling you to slow down or where to turn. Just you—and the freedom to go as far as your heart desires. You'll push beyond boundaries you never thought you could reach, discovering new potential at every step.

Now, imagine how you might live your life—free to run as far as you wish, with nothing and no one holding you back. Whether it's your career, your relationships, or any area of life you pursue, when you live without limiting beliefs, how far you go is entirely up to you.

Where will you go if the only limits are the ones you set for yourself? Like the runner on the beach, the only way to find out is to start running.

Day 2.
Observe, Do Nothing

"Observe the thought. Let it pass. Be still. Never poke the bear."

Not every thought needs your attention. Some appear suddenly, drift through the mind, and fade away just as quickly—if we let them. But the moment we engage, judge, or try to act on them, they grow louder. What was only temporary begins to take root. What could've moved past becomes persistent.

It's something I've learned again and again: when we react to every passing thought, we give it more power than it deserves. The strength to do nothing softens the noise. The quieter we become, the more clearly we can see—and the less judgmental thoughts bother us. As a former boss of mine used to say, "Don't poke the bear." He meant it playfully—but wisely. Some things are better left alone.

And that's true not just with other people—but with our own minds. Not every fear needs to be calmed. Not every emotion needs an explanation. Some thoughts are nomadic—just passing through. Let them.

And yet, in everyday life, we often do the opposite.

Sometimes we escalate things without even realizing it—by giving in to the urge to say the first thing that comes to mind. Even casual complaints—like grumbling about gas prices or what's on the news—often reflect deeper fears, and are best left unsaid.

I used to be quietly critical of others—especially people who seemed more successful. But those judgments weren't really about them. They were reflections of how I felt about myself. Every judgment was a mirror, and feeding those thoughts only deepened my own frustration.

That's the trouble with negative thoughts: they gain momentum. What begins as a fleeting emotion turns louder and heavier the more we engage. What could've passed quickly becomes something harder to manage. And that's why they're best observed—then left alone.

We must learn to coexist with our thoughts without letting them control us. Observe them—don't act on them, and don't speak them aloud. It's not the world around us that shapes how we feel—but how we interpret it. When we let our thoughts dictate our emotions and reactions, we become the source of our own struggle.

The solution is to manage your thoughts and reactions: resist the urge to act on them. Be with them. Feel them. But don't let them lead. Let the moment pass. Not everything needs a reaction—and you don't have to sacrifice your peace every time a thought demands your attention.

Observe what you're doing, but avoid engaging in thoughts or actions that leave you feeling worse, not better. When you can notice the urge to react and choose stillness instead, you take back your power—you decide how you feel, and what influences you.

We are not our thoughts—we are simply observing them. When we embrace that truth, we stop clinging to every opinion, fear, and judgment that passes through the mind. We let our thoughts come and go without needing to fix them. That's the quiet gift of observation: it loosens the grip of the stories we cling to and gives us room to breathe. Take a step back. Let things settle. Clarity has a way of finding you when you stop chasing it.

Thoughts come and go—that's just what they do. But that doesn't mean they all deserve your time. You don't have to solve them, follow them, or fear them. Just notice. Then let them move on.

The more you observe without reacting, the more you'll realize: most of what stresses you out isn't even real—it's just background noise on a channel you're not even watching.

Day 3.

Be Aware

---

*"Awareness keeps your hands off the hot stove—and
your mind out of the fire."*

Do you know what's going on around you? If you were
heading straight toward a wall, would you move out of the way
—or walk right into it? If you were in the right place at the
right time, with good things happening all around you, would
you even notice?

Most of us could learn to pay better attention to our
surroundings. Wouldn't it be nice to hit fewer speed bumps in
life? When we're truly present, we see more clearly: the
dangers to avoid, the opportunities to grab, and the joy that's
right in front of us.

Think back to a time when you hurt yourself because
you weren't paying attention. I can think of a few: slamming
my finger in a door, cutting myself with a peeling knife,
getting splashed with hot oil from a frying pan. All avoidable.
All the result of not being fully present in the moment.

From an early age, we're told to "pay attention." But over time, many of us stop thinking about what that actually means. At its core, paying attention is a survival instinct—when we stay aware of what we're doing, we're less likely to get hurt. That awareness keeps us safe, steady, and responsive to what's happening around us.

But it's not just about staying out of danger. Being present allows us to notice what others miss. We recognize when a friend's tone is off. We catch the small moments of peace between daily distractions. We see what needs our attention—and we have the clarity to respond.

Living with awareness brings peace—because we're prepared, not anxious. We don't get burned because we already know how close our hands are to the hot stove. We're not stressed about gas because we notice when the tank's getting low. We return to a clean home because we saw what needed tidying before we walked out the door.

Imagine a life where you're so aware of your surroundings that bills are paid weeks before they're due, groceries are purchased before they run out, and holiday shopping is always completed in plenty of time to relax. That's a life free of anxiety and stress. And maybe you're thinking, "But I don't have time to worry about every little thing." And for most of us, that's true. But being aware isn't about worrying over everything—it's about a life with very few worries at all, since you notice things before they become a problem

Of course, awareness comes more naturally to some than others—but the good news is, it's a learned skill, and anyone can improve it. Start by cutting out unnecessary distractions. Turn off the background noise. Put down the phone. Stop texting while doing other things. Practice giving your full attention to what's in front of you.

When we multitask, we believe we're being more efficient, but in reality, it just spreads our attention thin and results in lower-quality work. Pick one simple task—cooking dinner, driving to work, or folding laundry—and give it your full attention. When you focus on the present, your mind is free to process other thoughts that might otherwise get lost in the noise—thoughts that could reveal all kinds of ways to improve your life.

Being present in everything you do creates an environment of clarity. Of course, you can always return to multi-tasking after you master single-tasking; however, chances are that once you realize how enjoyable life is living in the moment, you won't ever want to go back—because living in the moment isn't just peaceful. It's proof that you're fully alive.

Day4.

React, Don't Be Reactive

"We can't control what comes our way—but we can write the story that follows."

It's normal to react when something triggers us—rude comments, surprise bills, traffic that makes you late. From a young age, we're taught to manage our emotions, especially anger. But the truth is, when something feels like a threat—whether to our pride, security, or sense of control—it's natural to want to strike back.

That's when the difference between reacting and being reactive becomes important.

When we react, we pause. We choose our next step. But when we're reactive, we don't think—we just respond. We lash out, shut down, or spiral into stress without considering the cost. In those moments, we surrender control to outside forces: people, problems, or emotions that have no business running the show.

It's not just about managing anger—it's about protecting our peace. Because when we're reactive, we end up causing ourselves more pain than the trigger ever did.

A friend of mine lived with a bully for decades. The pain was especially hard to escape because the bully was a close relative. It wore on him for years—so much so that he began putting himself down in his own mind, even long after the bully was out of the picture.

One day, he finally found peace. When I asked him what changed, he shared something powerful: "This person is a bully—that's their role, to tear people down. But I get to choose how I respond. I can't control what they did, but I can control how I let it affect me."

He realized that his own thoughts were doing more harm than the bully's words ever could. By taking control of his reactions, he freed himself from the bully's grip—and now, he's living a peaceful, fulfilling life.

By controlling our reactions, we gain mental and emotional freedom from the consequences of negative interactions. Instead of being pulled into someone else's chaos, we respond in ways that support our well-being—ways that bring clarity instead of confusion, peace instead of pain.

Remember, no one else can build you up 24/7/365— you have to do that yourself. Start by creating a mental barrier to outside influences and training your thoughts to work in your favor. Choose the way you respond, rather than reacting blindly. Begin by observing how you respond to situations in your life. Are you reacting, or being reactive? Here's a quick list to help you distinguish between the two:

REACTING

If you did any of the following, you were likely react**ing** mindfully, and not impulsively:

- I thought about my options *before* I reacted, and chose an action in my best interests.
- My response caused a desire for further engagement.
- My response caused happiness or excitement.
- My response sparked positive inspiration.

REACTIVE

In contrast, here's what being react**ive** might have looked like:

- I did *not* think about my options beforehand, and chose an action that did not benefit me.
- I acted impulsively.
- My response caused negative emotions (e.g., anxiety, grief).
- My response caused a negative physical reaction (e.g., nausea, perspiration, pain).

- My response caused regret for the action(s) I had done.

As you reflect on the list above, ask yourself honestly: Do I usually react with intention—or do I respond without thinking? Becoming aware of your patterns is the first step toward changing them. Remember, one of the key ingredients of true happiness is freedom from the influence of others. That kind of freedom starts when you take control of your reactions and protect your peace.

It's completely normal to respond to life's challenges— but when you pause and choose a response that supports your well-being, everything changes. You stop letting someone else's behavior determine your mood or peace of mind. You stop handing over control of how you feel. And that's when real growth begins.

From here on, let your responses reflect the life you want to create. Calm. Clear. Intentional. Choose wisely. That's how you stay in control.

Day 5.

Self-Love

"Self-love is the single greatest practice we can ever embrace."

Do you truly love yourself?

If you don't, it's time to start. Loving yourself is one of the most challenging things to master—but also one of the most rewarding.

You might be thinking, "Of course I love myself. I take care of my body, I eat well, I live a decent life." Or maybe you're thinking, "That's right—I do need to love myself more." No matter where you are in your journey, self-love is a lifelong practice that offers powerful returns. It has the ability to heal deep wounds, unlock personal growth, and give you access to real joy. On the flip side, when we don't love ourselves, life often feels like an uphill climb. We can still find moments of happiness, but they take more effort—and are often harder to hold onto.

So, what does it actually mean to love yourself? It means putting your well-being first. It means meeting your needs, enjoying your life, and looking forward to each new day —not just surviving it.

Here are a few quick questions to find out if this is the life you're living:

- Are your nutritional and physical needs met?

- Are you emotionally steady, with mostly positive thoughts and peaceful sleep?

- Is your stress manageable?

- Are your relationships healthy and respectful?

- Does the thought of a new day excite you?

If you can't confidently say "yes" to all of these, that's okay. Self-love is a process—and any place you start is the right place to begin. Choosing to improve how you care for yourself is already a powerful act of love.

Of course, challenges will still show up. No one is immune to surprise setbacks or stressful days. But self-love makes those moments easier to handle—and they tend to affect you less when you've made your well-being a priority. If today's reflection shows you where there's room to grow, lean into it. Just remember: even a small shift in how you treat yourself can lead to meaningful change.

Try planting simple reminders to do something for yourself around your home—whether it's a sticky note on the mirror, a voice memo, or a memento that helps you pause and reflect. Taking care of yourself is something you build through consistent, intentional choices. Here are a few ways to start:

Practice Self-Care
Prioritize your physical needs: get enough rest, eat nutritious meals, and stay active. These are the basics of honoring your body.

Practice Mindfulness
Be present with how you spend your time. Notice what brings you joy and what drains you. Let go of judgment and stay grounded in the moment.

Set Boundaries
Protect your time and energy. Surround yourself with people and places that bring you joy—and don't be afraid to say "no" when it matters.

Be Kind to Yourself
Practice compassion. Laugh at your mistakes, forgive yourself quickly, and become your own greatest encourager.

Many of us were taught to always put others first—to sacrifice, to serve, to keep giving. We're told that actions of self-care are "selfish" or "stingy." But there's a huge difference between being selfish and taking care of yourself. You've likely heard the saying, "You can't pour from an empty cup." This is true in every way. It's why airlines instruct passengers to put on their own oxygen mask before helping others. Because in order to be of real service to the people we love, we first have to take care of ourselves.

Behind every great leader is someone who knows how to tend to their needs and stay connected to their own purpose. That's what allows them to show up for others. And when you love yourself, people around you start to take notice. Those who don't respect that may naturally fade away. Over time, your life becomes filled with people who share that same level of self-respect—and they'll support you in the most amazing ways.

So give yourself the gift of self-love today. It's one of the greatest blessings you'll ever receive.

Day 6.

Stay in the Moment

"The past is memory. The future is imagination. Right here, right now is the only true control we ever have."

We all carry pieces of the past with us. Some memories lift us—moments with loved ones that still make us smile, places we miss, or chapters of ourselves we've moved on from. Others remind us of pain: childhood wounds, failed relationships, or identities we've left behind. These memories live within us, often resurfacing when we least expect them— showing up as emotion, hesitation, or old stories we've told ourselves for far too long.

Sometimes, we get stuck in those memories. Even the good ones can pull us away from the life unfolding right in front of us. And when we spend too much time in the past— replaying what was or reliving what hurt—we miss the peace and fulfillment that only exist in the present.

And just like the past can trap us, the future can too. Even when our thoughts are hopeful, spending too much time in "what's next" leads to anxious questions: *What if something goes wrong? What if I can't do this? What if it doesn't work out?* But worrying about the future doesn't lead to better decisions. After all, what good does it do to fear what's coming when we have the power to shape it by focusing on today?

The only true place where we have control is right here, right now. The past is gone, and the future hasn't arrived. When we stay in the moment, we avoid the consequences of the "What if's" and "If only's."

This doesn't mean you shouldn't plan for the future. It simply means that while you have your plans, your thoughts should stay focused on the present. What you do today shapes what's to come. Life is always changing, so we must take the driver's seat. If we don't, who's steering our course? A friend once told me, *"Things can't stay like this forever; everything changes. That's just how it works."* He was right. Life is like a hiking trail—sometimes rocky, sometimes smooth. But one thing's for sure: it's never constant. If we stay mindful of where we step, we'll walk the smoothest paths.

Being present helps reduce stress, anxiety, guilt, and worry—all of which tend to arise when our minds drift away from the moment. When we focus on what's right in front of us, we interrupt the spiral of overthinking. We make better choices. We feel more grounded. The more we practice presence, the more resilient, calm, and connected we become —even in the middle of a busy or hectic day.

Staying in the moment is not always easy, especially with a world full of distractions pulling us in every direction. But it's possible to train your mind to focus on what's right in front of you. Start small by incorporating brief moments of mindfulness into your day. For example, when you're drinking your morning coffee, notice the warmth of the cup, the aroma, the simple act of sipping. This small practice of paying attention to the present can help break the cycle of overthinking and give your mind a chance to reset.

Staying present isn't just for quiet moments of solitude —it's a practice that can be applied in even the most chaotic of situations. Take a challenging conversation, for instance. When emotions run high, it's easy for our minds to race ahead —thinking about what we'll say next, or replaying what's already been said. Instead, try focusing on listening fully to the other person's words and emotions. By staying in the moment, you not only respond with more clarity and empathy, but you also avoid saying things you might regret.

Similarly, in high-pressure work situations, it's easy to get caught up in future outcomes—worrying about deadlines, performance, or expectations. But when we stay focused on the task at hand, we perform better and reduce the chances of getting overwhelmed. One step at a time, one moment at a time, is often all it takes to navigate stressful circumstances more smoothly.

Another powerful way to stay in the moment is to check in with your breath. When you feel your thoughts drifting toward the past or future, take a few deep breaths. Inhale slowly for four counts. Hold for four. Exhale for four. Repeat a few times. This simple rhythm not only settles your nervous system—it brings you back to the here and now.

When you find yourself getting lost in thoughts of "What if?" or "If only," gently redirect your focus. Remind yourself that the present is where life is happening. Whether you're enjoying a conversation with a friend, working on a task, or simply walking down the street, these moments are what truly matter. By continuously bringing yourself back to the present, you become shielded from the stress that comes with living in the past or future.

Train yourself to stay in the moment. It's a foundational practice for peace of mind and a proven tool for staying grounded. I'd love to tell you how long I've been practicing this, but honestly, I don't think about it much anymore. Right now, I'm staying in the moment. Won't you give it a try?

Day 7.

With Everything, Go Inward

"Once you master the art of going inward, nothing can overpower your thoughts—and you finally step into the role of creator."

Meditation works—because it quiets the mind, resets your thoughts, and brings your focus inward. In a world full of noise and distraction, this simple act of stillness can be life-changing.

But how does it actually work?

When we meditate, we interrupt the constant stream of thoughts—both the helpful and harmful ones. You might ask, "Why stop the good thoughts too?"

Think of it like restarting a sluggish computer. Even if your favorite programs seem to be running fine, the system still benefits from a clean reset.

Meditation works the same way. It clears mental clutter so your mind can run more smoothly. It creates space for clarity, peace, and insight—the kind that gets drowned out by everything pulling on your attention.

Meditation is a blessing in that it provides us with a way to turn off external distractions—both the ones we're aware of and those we're not. It helps us reclaim control over our thoughts, especially in a world full of interruptions. Too often, we're guided by external influences—co-workers, family, social media, the news. These "influencers" shape the way we think. As many great meditators, teachers, and spiritual leaders say: truth reveals itself when we allow it to surface. Even if meditation feels unfamiliar, simply learning to be still—free from distractions—can help you hear your inner wisdom without all the noise.

I used to think meditation was something reserved for monks or yogis with endless free time. It felt out of reach, unnecessary, and strange—until I tried it. At first, I could barely sit still for five minutes. But I kept showing up, and over time, something shifted. The peace I'd so desperately needed? I started to find it in those quiet moments. And that's when I found the answers I was looking for.

Start by taking moments to go inward. The answers may not come immediately, but over time, with practice, they will. Once you master the art of going inward, no task or concept can overpower your thoughts, and you step into the role of creator. Even if you can't understand everything (and you won't), stillness reveals that complete understanding isn't always possible. This helps you release the need to know, which is a form of freedom from control.

Pause and ask yourself: What would life look like with true mental, emotional, and spiritual freedom?

Here are just a few things you may experience through meditation and stillness:

- **Peace of mind**
  A quieting of the thoughts that fuel anxiety, fear, grief, and worry.
- **Mental clarity**
  The ability to focus on thoughts that bring peace, while easily releasing those that distract or weigh you down.
- **Intentional focus**
  Choosing which thoughts to engage with—and which to gently let go.
- **A calmer body**
  As the mind slows, so does the heart. A steady calm begins to carry into your actions.
- **Aligned attention**
  Your energy becomes focused and directed, rather than scattered or reactive.

- **Emotional regulation**
  You respond rather than react, gaining greater ease with your moods and behaviors.
- **Joy in the ordinary**
  Presence turns simple moments—like folding laundry or washing dishes—into quiet, joyful experiences.

If you're new to meditation, start simple. Find a quiet space, sit comfortably, close your eyes, and focus on your breath. Inhale slowly through your nose. Hold. Exhale gently through your mouth. If your mind wanders, just notice —and return to your breath. No judgment, no pressure. Even a few minutes a day can begin to shift the way you think and feel. Make stillness your goal. Go slow, and enjoy the experience.

There are endless resources—apps, guided recordings, videos—but the most powerful tool is your willingness to begin. Keep it light, keep it consistent, and let it evolve in your own time.

And above all, remember: with everything, go inward. The more you listen, the more you'll realize—you've carried the answers all along. Meditation simply helps you hear them.

Day 8.

Realize Your Power

---

*"When you control how you think, act, and feel—you're
in the driver's seat of your life."*

Do you realize just how powerful you are?

And no, this isn't about leaping across the Grand Canyon or melting steel with your eyes. This is about the true power you hold over the creation of your life. You have the power to shape your emotions, to choose how you feel, and in doing so, you choose how you live each day. You have the power to experience consistent happiness and live free of fear, worry, anxiety, or guilt. This means you have the power to create your own world. Few ever come to realize this in their lifetime—and if you do, you are truly blessed.

Once this was a little-known secret. Today, more and more people are discovering this priceless tool for taking charge of their experiences. How? It's simple: if you control how you think, act, and feel, you are in the driver's seat of your everyday life. Happiness is yours for the taking, and joy and peace may be found in almost everything you do. Sound too good to be true? This is called self-mastery, a pursuit that countless individuals have been chasing since the beginning of time.

What is self-mastery? It's having control over your thoughts—meaning you choose whether to feel happy, sad, stressed, or joyful. How do you achieve it? By first consciously choosing to take control of your experiences. When you realize your reactions are a choice, you begin to choose healthier ones —something that becomes easier when you view your experiences through a lens of your own design. That's how you decide how you see the world.

I recall many times when life felt completely out of my hands—like I was just reacting instead of living. For years, it was like being on a ride I never signed up for, just holding on for dear life. Then one day, I caught myself against a wall and thought, "Why am I letting this ruin my day?" That moment changed everything. I realized I had a choice. I could keep surrendering to my thoughts—or I could take back control. It wasn't instant, but that shift sparked something in me: the beginning of personal-mastery.

The tools in this book outline how to choose happiness and joy, even in the face of challenges and despair. It's a matter of perception and understanding that everything is an opportunity to grow and expand. But before you master changing your perceptions, first realize that you do have control over them.

To begin, start noticing your current observations as you go about your day. Pay attention to how you view things, and make a conscious effort to avoid engaging in pessimistic internal dialogue—no matter the situation. This shift in perception is the first step toward personal mastery. Just as you've learned to walk or brush your teeth without thinking, you can also train your mind to choose positive thoughts with the same ease. The more you practice, the more natural it becomes. This is the path of personal mastery: learning to choose happiness, again and again. Once you realize that happiness is a choice, the next steps unfold with clarity and ease.

You deserve to experience happiness, love, and joy every day. The first step is simple: recognize that the power to create that experience has always been within you. When you take ownership of your thoughts and actions, happiness stops feeling like something distant—and starts feeling like home. With consistency and care, it becomes a way of life.

Day 9.

Transmute Your Problems

*"Changing your thoughts doesn't just change your mind
—it changes everything."*

"Transmute" is a popular term in spiritual, religious, and self-help communities, but it can easily apply to any area where something negative needs to be transformed into something positive. If you're new to the concept, it's about taking something that affects you poorly (like stress) and transforming it into something positive (like happiness). Let's take a closer look.

"Transmute" = "trans" + "mute." "Trans" means to transfer, change location, or move from one place to another, while "mute" means to silence—like muting the television, turning off the noise. So, we learn to "transmute" the inner voices of stress, anxiety, worry, and torment by "moving" those thoughts to a new place and "muting" their nagging words.

How do we do this? We begin by practicing inner work —using techniques like the ones in this book—to examine and release our attachment to negative thought patterns and beliefs. When we do this, we interrupt the constant loop of nagging thoughts and make space for ones that are more positive, loving, and empowering. It's not always easy at first, as quieting our inner commentary or resetting nagging thoughts can feel like a challenge. But with practice, it becomes an essential skill for cultivating a peaceful and joyful life.

Here are a few tips for transmuting negative thought patterns:

1. **Be Aware:** The first step in transforming negative thoughts is recognizing them. Becoming mindful of emotions like stress, self-doubt, fear, or anxiety is crucial. Simply being aware of your thoughts can be a powerful tool in taking back control.

2. **Observe:** Instead of reacting immediately to a negative thought, try taking a moment to observe it. Acknowledge it without judgment by saying, "I'm having a negative thought," or "I'm feeling stressed." This helps you detach from the automatic emotional responses and lets you view the thought more objectively.

3. **Pause:** Take a deep breath and pause. It helps clear your mind and signals to your body that there's no

immediate threat. Pausing interrupts the cycle of negative thoughts and gives you a moment to reset.

4. **Redirect:** Redirect the negative thought with a positive one. For example, if you're feeling stressed about a presentation, affirm to yourself, "I am prepared, confident, and capable," and visualize a successful outcome. Shifting your mindset like this directs your energy toward success.

Transmutation is a conscious act—dissolving unwanted emotions and replacing them with ones we enjoy and prefer. When you start replacing negative thoughts with positive ones, you'll immediately feel a shift in your energy and mood. The result is a healthier, happier life.

You deserve thoughts that bring you peace, not stress—joy, not fear. The moment you begin choosing better thoughts, your entire life begins to shift. Do it for yourself, out of love and the desire to improve your life. Remember, the journey of a thousand miles begins with a single step. Take that first step toward a better, more fulfilling life. Ask yourself: Isn't it time?

Day 10.

The Calm Before the... Calm

"Peace isn't found after the storm has passed—it comes from the journey inside it."

It's a peaceful evening on the water. The boat rocks gently from side to side, soothing, as the sun fades to horizontal red, orange, and yellow lines of sunset pastels. It's the calm before the storm.

We've all heard the expression—and maybe even used it ourselves: "the calm before the storm." Perhaps you've walked into a store or business, asked, "Slow day?" only to have the employees quickly hush you, as if saying the words aloud will disrupt the calm and bring in an unexpected rush of customers. This anxiety, this fear of the storm that's about to hit, often has us bracing for pain we don't even know is coming. But what does that mindset really get us? Fear, anxiety, worry... Does it serve us? Not at all.

Storms come. A forgotten bill, a broken appliance, a root canal, the loss of a pet... these things happen. What matters most is how we handle them. Do we live in fear of what's coming? Do we fill the days leading up to an inevitable storm with dread and anxiety? How we prepare for life's challenges—and how we move through them—shapes the peace we experience, and whether we allow dis-ease to settle in.

So, how do we train ourselves to not focus on the approaching storms? You might be thinking, "How can I ignore it when I know it's coming? I can't just pretend it's not there. I'm not going to bury my head in the sand." Of course not. But here's something I learned long ago when I worked for a gardener, tending to high-end homes in the mountains. We did all kinds of jobs, from pruning delicate roses to clearing thick briars and overgrown foliage. One day, while we were knee-deep in kudzu during the summer heat, I asked my boss, "Do you ever see any snakes when you're working out here?"

"No," he said. "I don't look for them."

At the time, I thought his answer was silly—almost frustrating. I was definitely looking out for them! Later that day, I nearly stepped on a black snake, actually stepped on a brown one, and ended up leaving work early after I startled a rattlesnake that had been hiding right beside me.

What's the lesson here? Well, sure, don't wade too deep in kudzu—but seriously, we all know there are things in life that cause us anxiety. We know that storms are brewing somewhere, and from time to time, we will get caught in them.

The key is to live with the awareness that tough times are inevitable—but we can choose not to focus all our energy on them. You must know that nothing will come your way that you can't handle. And once you get through the storm, you're wiser and tougher, which means the next storm will bother you less. Yes, snakes hide in tall grass—but we tend to find more of them when we go looking for trouble.

Don't focus on what's ahead. Whenever a challenge arises, try saying one of these affirmations out loud—or silently to yourself:

- I can handle this. I can handle anything.
- This is an opportunity to become a wiser, more capable person.
- I will grow from this.
- I am a wise, creative individual, and this is no problem for me.
- From experience, I know this cannot last.

Life throws lemons at us, whether we have wealth or not, education or not, opportunities or not. They will come, occasionally, whether we fear them or not. But understanding this gives us the foresight to choose a reality of peace.

Instead of dreading the ripples ahead, we can learn to flow with calmness. With a little practice, our perception of "storms" can shift entirely, until one day, we may find ourselves living in the calm before the... calm.

Day 11.

Grace Is Always an Option

"Grace is strength wrapped in tenderness—it's how we rise with love, especially when we feel broken."

Have you ever felt humiliated? The flush of embarrassment when you're exposed in front of others—when you share a secret or intimate detail, only to have it received in a way you didn't intend? Or maybe you've been made to feel guilty or ashamed for simply being yourself?

Imagine this scenario: your employer calls you into their office. They acknowledge your hard work, telling you they can't ask for more because you're already giving everything you've got. But despite your best efforts, your performance still isn't meeting expectations. They explain that the job requires more than you're able to give, and that you're not adding the value they need. You're given two weeks to find a new job, a new income stream—a new you.

It would be difficult, if not impossible, to avoid sinking into sadness or depression. And even more challenging to not direct anger towards yourself, or worse, someone else.

Situations like this strip us of our emotional sovereignty—the ability to control how we feel. When we lose this control, our emotions take the reins, often leading us into a downward spiral. In moments like these, when our emotions threaten to overwhelm us, grace is the tool we can use to regain control.

So, what exactly is "grace"? Grace is elegance. It's ease. The phrase "saving grace" refers to a redeeming quality—how running became her saving grace during a tough transition, or how faith was his saving grace after losing a loved one. "Amazing Grace," as we know, is both a hymn and a symbol of divine love and kindness that transcends all other emotions. Grace is what we hold on to when we need a helping hand.

To act with grace, then, means to behave in a way that preserves self-love and nurtures our mental, physical, and emotional well-being. Grace is a shield we use to protect ourselves in times of despair, when our thoughts or emotions can easily fall to the wayside. It isn't about suppressing emotions; it's about choosing how we respond, and doing so in a way that maintains our emotional sovereignty.

Now, can you imagine, in this difficult situation, expressing gratitude to your employer for the opportunity and the experiences you've had? You rise, shake hands, and quietly walk to the door. Reacting with anger or bitterness won't help —you'd only drag yourself deeper into distress. When you approach difficult situations with kindness, remember this: Although your kind words may be spoken to someone else, the person they heal most is you. Your boss might not even notice your grace, but the emotions you feel when you choose kindness will linger far longer, easing some of the anger, frustration, or sadness.

Our emotions exist only in our own reality. Others can't feel them the way we do. This is why it's so important to protect our own emotional well-being, because no one else can do it for us. And we do this by choosing grace in every situation. Grace is almost always the best option for long-term health. It isn't just gentle on the mind and body; Grace is a healing force that helps replace negative emotional states with more positive, lasting ones.

We can't control how others behave—but we can choose how we respond. That's why it's essential to protect our emotional sovereignty: the power to decide how we feel, no matter the circumstances. One of the most powerful ways to do that is through grace. Choose it whenever you can. Grace nurtures your well-being, transforms hardship, and gently leads you toward a more peaceful, fulfilling life.

Day 12.

Letting Go

"When we let go of excess baggage, we literally—and figuratively—feel lighter."

Letting go is hard—because we're wired to hold on. We cling to the past, to memories, to what once felt safe or familiar. Letting go requires change—a leap into the unknown, toward an outcome we can't fully predict. If it came naturally, we wouldn't need to work at it. But it doesn't—so we sometimes carry baggage that lingers. We hold on, even when it hurts. And yet, releasing that weight is often the most loving thing we can do for ourselves.

I can point to some of the hardest things I've ever had to let go of:

1. **People**—the ones whose departure left me overwhelmed with grief or, at times, with too much love and no one to share it with. The loss of my mother and the disappointment of a failed marriage are among the most difficult.

2. **The loss of identity**—careers that once defined me, until one day, they no longer did.

3. **The loss of ideas**—particularly the belief that I would be *[fill in your own vision]*, because it depended on someone or something that could never be. For example, the idea that I would be a happily married spouse with two and a half kids, living the traditional dream.

Now, think about a heavy attachment you've released. Don't get lost in the details or dwell on the past. Remember, we can acknowledge our growth without re-traumatizing ourselves by revisiting those painful moments. Ask yourself: *Was letting go difficult? Did this attachment control your life until you set it free?* Perhaps this attachment hasn't completely gone, but you know it needs to. *Are you holding on to anything right now that you need to release?* Most of us are. Identifying these attachments is the first step toward creating a life where they no longer hold us back. You can do it —like anything, you just need to know how.

Here's how to start:

1. **Recognize the attachment that needs to be released.** Reflection and honesty are essential. The first step is acknowledging that something needs to be let go. No one can do this work for you

—you must be honest with yourself to begin healing.

2. **Explore the cause of the attachment**

   Understand the source of the attachment. Why did it originate? How has it shaped who you are today?

3. **Forgive yourself or others**

   We are all human, with all our divine complexity. Our attention is one of the most powerful tools we have for creating the life we want. Forgive yourself for the attention you've given to this attachment and any impact it may have had on your life. Forgive yourself for anything you've said or done related to it. Let the past rest.

4. **Re-shift your attention**

   Shifting your focus is key. You can do this by visualizing a life without the attachment—whether in your journal, in your mind, or aloud. Picture how everything could change once the attachment is released.

5. **Reset your mind**

   Use meditation or stillness to reset your thoughts and refocus your energy.

6. **Seek help**

   We live in a time where help is available everywhere. If your attachment is causing emotional, psychological, or physical harm, seek professional help immediately. This book isn't an exhaustive healing resource, but it can help you identify areas that need attention.

Whether you're looking to shed twenty-five pounds or release nagging thought patterns, letting go can set you free. Our bodies—physical, emotional, and spiritual—feel lighter when we release what no longer serves us.

Think of a time when you traveled. A suitcase is useful for carrying your clothing and personal items to your destination, but would you want to carry it with you the entire time? Not likely. It's always a better experience when our baggage stays in the room.

When we let go of excess baggage, we literally—and figuratively—feel lighter. Feeling lighter, whether in our thoughts, hearts, or bodies, gives us the freedom to think clearly, live without restrictions, and experience a better life.

Letting go doesn't mean forgetting—it means moving forward with peace. It's time to let go.

Your next chapter is waiting.

Day 13.

If You Have Love, You Are Rich

"Love—real, unconditional love—is the only thing that never fades."

Inside the office building, behind a large desk, sits Carmen, neat and well-dressed as she is every day of the week. Her smile and attention to detail in her appearance demand respect, and her nameplate carries the admirable title of "Office Manager."

One day, Carmen confessed that behind her smile there is disdain for the high-salaried individuals she is polite to, forcing herself to spout "yes ma'ams" and "no sirs" to all the many customers she encounters from families of means. On this day, she smiled at a young man who saw right through her facade. He was on his last penny, but Carmen didn't know it. He gently asked, "What's wrong?" and to her own surprise, Carmen began to weep.

"Do you have family?" the young man continued. "Someone, or maybe even a pet, who waits for you at home, because the moment they've been living for all day is the moment you come back into their lives."

Carmen continued to weep, nodding her head vigorously up and down.

"Well," said the young man. "If you have love, you are rich."

The young man, having lost nearly everyone he ever loved, just learned this himself. Carmen, moved by the authenticity and sincerity in his voice, knew this to be true.

That night, she returned home, greeted her family with warm hugs—and more tears.

"What's wrong?" asked her husband.

"I have love, and I am rich because of it," replied Carmen, and she meant it.

Later that night, as she lay in bed, she thought to herself, "In all that you do—whether it's love for yourself or love from another—if you have love, you are rich. I have love. And I am rich."

Carmen smiled and slept very well.

You see, as cliché as it sounds, no salary, streaming television show, or political candidate will ever leave you feeling fulfilled all the time. Once the show ends or the news cycle moves on, the feeling fades, and you find yourself looking for the next object of attention. Love, though— unconditional love—will always be there. Love for yourself, love for family, love for a pet—it doesn't matter. It's the one constant that never fades.

If you find yourself living in a constant state of lack, of wanting more fulfillment, it may indicate that love is missing from your life. What areas of your life would benefit from more love? What would you be open to changing to invite more love in? Would you like to love yourself more? Would you consider having a pet to share your life with?

Recognizing where there is room for more love is a key step in creating the life you desire. Spend time reflecting on this, and keep it in mind as you move through the pages of this book. The tools you acquire here will help you fill your "love tank" with the fuel you need to get where you're going—and perhaps for the first time, that destination is you.

Day 14.

Be a Kid Again

"Think back to the last time you did something that made your heart smile. That joy? You still deserve it— every day."

Be a kid again. And no, we're not talking about playing hooky or eating Happy Meals (although, that may sound fun). We're talking about reconnecting with the playful spirit inside you—the part of you that craves the activities that make you smile, the ones that remind you of what it felt like to live carefree. When you were so immersed in fun that you forgot everything else—no matter how big, small, or heavy it was.

Think for a moment: When was the last time you did something like that?

Children get so lost in their imagination that they're completely oblivious to the world around them. Call out, "Time for dinner!" and they might not hear you—because they're so caught up in their play. How many times did you hear your name called before you snapped out of it as a kid? Probably more than once!

As children, we instinctively understand the value of fun, and we lose ourselves in play, tuning out the rest of the world. It's an experience we, as adults, often forget is even possible. Unfortunately, as we grow older, we tend to lose touch with that playful, creative side of life. The good news? We can reconnect with that child inside us, and doing so can truly transform our lives.

Can you remember the last time you did something simply because you loved doing it? When you were so absorbed in the joy of it that nothing—and no one—could pull you away? That's the kind of joy you need in your life. It's therapeutic.

As adults, we often find ourselves doing things because we feel we *must*—chores, work, or filling time with activities like watching television, scrolling through social media, or aimlessly browsing the internet. The sad reality is that in these moments, we're letting our lives—our opportunities, our experiences—slip by.

Even when we're not just "passing time," most of us still dedicate large chunks of our lives to life's demands—jobs, school, taking care of others... While it's important to earn a living and support our families, if we don't make room for joy, the weight of responsibility can throw our lives completely out of balance.

What if, instead, your life could be in harmony? What if joy and commitment could coexist? How would it feel to wake up each day, renewed, filled with happiness, simply because you're alive? We can find that balance—if we prioritize joy.

Take a moment to reflect on how you're spending your time. Are there moments in your week that feel joyful—or are most of them just passing by? If it helps, journal about what truly lights you up. Then, gently begin reintroducing small activities that bring you joy—whether it's something new or something you once loved. Just like you did as a child, you can use your imagination to turn even ordinary moments into something meaningful. The key is to make space for what makes you feel alive.

Incorporating joy into your routine, even in small ways, will ripple out into other areas of your life. Before you know it, childlike excitement will infuse everything you do. It's simple—you just need to give yourself permission to be a kid again.

When the child within us is allowed to emerge, we reconnect with joy, happiness, and fun. Doing this—even just once a week—will bring the kind of happiness many of us are missing. Pure joy—the kind that kids experience, even in small doses—goes a long way. It can sustain us through even the darkest times.

By embracing that playful spirit, we unlock a life full of creativity, happiness, and the kind of joy that many of us haven't felt since childhood. Start today and discover how good it feels to be a kid again!

Joy isn't just for kids—it's for all of us, in every stage, season, and circumstance of life. You're never too old to feel light, playful, and free.

Day 15.

Fall in Love with Yourself

---

*"Self-love is the result of truly knowing yourself—and
learning to love what you find."*

The fastest route to a happy life is to fall in love with yourself.

It's true. No one will ever know you more fully than you know yourself. So, loving yourself is by far the most authentic and true form of love you'll ever experience—think about it.

Now, ask yourself: Do I love who I am? Do I love all that I am and all that I do, "warts and all," as they say?

For most of us, the answer is a silent—and sometimes not so silent—"No!" But it doesn't have to be, and it shouldn't be. Falling in love with yourself is simpler than it sounds. Sure, it doesn't always come naturally, but the path to self-love can begin at any time. It starts with a few simple steps: **slow down, and experience everything.**

How do we slow down? We turn off the critical voice in our minds—the inner commentary that distracts us, causes us to lose focus, and pulls us out of the present moment. When we stop overthinking, we become present in the moment and fully aware of what's going on around us.

How do we experience everything? By paying attention! Living in the moment allows us to be fully aware of our thoughts and actions, free from distractions. Through this presence, we can experience everything—fully and authentically.

The truth is: loving yourself is something anyone can do. It's not about being perfect, but about showing yourself the same compassion you would show a close friend. When you make a mistake or feel low, it's easy to fall into the trap of self-criticism. But self-love begins when you can pause, take a breath, and treat yourself with the kindness you deserve. It's about embracing your flaws, understanding that they don't define you, and offering yourself the same gentle encouragement you'd offer someone you love. This self-compassion becomes the foundation for all the other steps of self-love, allowing you to move forward with a heart that is open and forgiving, not harsh and judgmental.

Remember, falling in love with yourself doesn't happen overnight, and it doesn't need to be all at once. It's a gradual process, built from many small actions and shifts in perspective. Each kind word you say to yourself, each moment you choose self-compassion, and each time you embrace your imperfections—all of these moments add up. Over time, they transform the way you see yourself, until one day you realize just how far you've come.

Falling in love with yourself means being present with who you are—fully and intentionally. And one of the best ways to cultivate this presence is by living in the moment. When we are truly engaged with the here and now, we stop getting lost in the past or worrying about the future. It's in these moments of presence that we begin to understand ourselves better and experience life with all its richness.

Living in the moment brings countless benefits—so many, in fact, it could fill an entire book. But for now, know this: one of the most important results is that it helps us get to know ourselves. We cultivate self-love by truly understanding ourselves—by being an active participant in our decisions and experiences, rather than just going through the motions. When we engage intentionally with our lives, we naturally begin to choose the experiences that bring us joy.

How often do you consciously decide what you do? How often do you live on autopilot? Do you actively choose where to eat, what to do in your free time, or where to go? When we slow down, we regain control over the choices we make, and we tend to choose what makes us smile. This allows us to enjoy the process of life. After slowing down just a few times, many quickly realize how beneficial it is and find it hard to go back.

When we practice self-love, we inevitably discover more opportunities for happiness in our everyday lives. We might rearrange our home, change our appearance, take on new hobbies, or even make new friends. Life is a process, and it's meant to be enjoyed. Remember to smile and laugh.

This is the journey of life: it isn't about getting it right the first time—and it never will be. Once we understand this, we begin to laugh at the missteps, the lessons, and even the unexpected wins. Because growth isn't about perfection—it's about showing up, trying again, and learning as we go.

Too often, we dismiss the idea of self-love because we believe it's impossible or that there's nothing to love. But this is a learned misconception, and it's simply not true. We cultivate self-love by creating experiences that make life as enjoyable as possible. Start with small things: groceries you enjoy, a fresh new look, a walk outside—and slow down to savor each moment. Before long, you'll find yourself living and loving life in the present.

This is how you fall in love with yourself—not all at once, but moment by moment. Just keep moving toward yourself. Soon, you'll become your own greatest admirer.

And when you do, you'll wonder why you ever accepted anything less than the love you now give yourself.

Day 16.

Customize Your Thoughts

"If we can choose how our outer world looks, we can also choose how our inner world feels."

We love custom options. From our coffee orders to our playlists, everything these days is tailored to reflect our preferences—and we've come to expect it. Our cars, homes, phones, and even our jobs are curated to suit our tastes. We do this because customization gives us a sense of control. It reflects who we are, and we associate that with happiness.

But what about the world inside us? What about the thoughts we think every day—the ones that shape how we feel, how we show up, and how we experience our lives? Isn't that worth crafting with just as much care?

Here's the good news: you can customize your thoughts, too. With a little practice you can design a mental space that supports joy, peace, and clarity—just like a beautifully curated home, only this one lives inside you. A space where your thoughts feel comforting, your emotions feel supported, and your mind becomes a place you actually want to spend time.

Think about it: What good is a beautiful house, car, or outfit if your inner world feels restless, critical, or disconnected? What's the point of perfect aesthetics if your mind doesn't feel like a place you actually want to live in? Customization isn't just about appearances—it's about creating environments that help us thrive.

Try this: Picture the home you live in—the place where you rest, reset, and recharge. Is it peaceful? Comfortable? When your space supports your well-being, it affects how you show up in the world. A good night's sleep, a nourishing meal, or a cozy moment of stillness can set the tone for an entire day. Your mind works the same way.

Empowering thoughts are like a restful home: they energize you, ground you, and make space for joy. Unhealthy thoughts, on the other hand, are like living in a house that looks great on the outside but feels hollow on the inside— unsettling, uncomfortable, and draining. The interior matters.

If we want to feel less overwhelmed by stress, fear, or doubt, we must begin within. Just as we fine-tune the outer world to fit our needs, we can fine-tune our minds through inner work—the process of creating clarity, healing, and conscious choice.

When we don't customize our thoughts, they run on default settings—many of which were programmed by fear, past experiences, or the opinions of others. These old, unexamined patterns shape how we see ourselves and the world, often without us even realizing it. We react instead of respond. We settle instead of choose. Over time, this creates an inner environment that feels cluttered, chaotic, or even hostile. We begin to believe the noise in our heads without questioning if it's true—or if it even belongs to us. And just like living in a home that doesn't reflect who you are, you start to feel disconnected from yourself.

So how do we do it? How do we design an inner world that reflects the peace and joy we long for? The answer is simple: we customize. We keep what we love and shift what no longer serves us.

Inner work helps us unlearn old thought patterns and replace them with new ones—ones that reflect the person we're becoming, not the version we've outgrown. There are many ways to do this: meditation, therapy, mindfulness, spiritual practice, journaling, or simply asking ourselves better questions.

Being here now, reading this book, and reflecting on these ideas—that's part of your inner work. By learning how you feel and why, you're taking ownership of your experience. You're choosing to reshape what you think and believe, which ultimately changes how you feel and live.

Just imagine if you gave your inner world the same energy, creativity, and care you give to your outer one. With a little focus, even small shifts in how you think can help shape your thoughts into a space that feels calm, clear, and aligned with the person you want to become. You'll begin to unlearn what doesn't serve you, and build something new from the inside out.

Your inner world is the most sacred space you have. It's where everything begins. Why not make it a place you're proud to live in?

Day 17.

Identify Dualities

"Dualities are distractions that weigh us down. Free yourself from their hold, and you'll discover a world of new possibilities."

Have you ever noticed the warning on car side mirrors that says, "Objects in mirror are closer than they appear"? This message is designed to remind us that what we see isn't always the full picture—it's magnified and closer than we may realize. Now, imagine we had a similar tool for our everyday lives. What if we had a way to identify potentially unhealthy situations before they even became a problem? How much more control would we feel over our decisions and peace of mind?

One powerful method for gaining that clarity and control is recognizing dualities in your thinking.

Dualities are essentially opposing or contrasting ideas, where one cannot exist without the other—think light and dark, good and bad, right and wrong. These dualities often show up in our minds as distractions, pulling our attention away from the present moment and causing unnecessary stress. They often present themselves as either/or choices that can feel like we're stuck in frustrating "darned if you do, darned if you don't" situations. They can be simple, even mundane choices—yet they create mental tension that feels much bigger than it is:

- If I use some of my time off—I won't have enough left for later
- Should I speak up—or stay silent
- Do I go—or stay
- Do I buy this—or not
- Are they upset—or am I overthinking it
- Do I work now—or take a break

If you've ever found yourself stuck between two options, second-guessing every move—you're not alone. Dualities have a way of making life feel more complicated than it actually is. They stir up anxiety and trick us into thinking we're one decision away from messing everything up. But most of the time, that's just not true.

The thing about dualities is that they limit our choices and can lead us into unhealthy mental patterns. If we aren't careful, they can create unnecessary stress, anxiety, and confusion. When we get caught up in dualistic thinking, we oversimplify situations that have more layers than appear. Life is rarely as simple as "this or that"—most decisions involve multiple perspectives, and narrowing them down to just two options often leaves us feeling stuck or overwhelmed. It's easy to slip into an "all-or-nothing" mindset, thinking that every decision is make-or-break, but that approach doesn't serve us well in the long run.

What's more, when we frame life as "right or wrong," we tend to create unnecessary conflicts with others. We can end up seeing people as either agreeing with us or opposing us, which closes the door to meaningful connections and opens the door to division. Dualistic thinking can also leave us constantly striving for perfection and, as a result, missing out on opportunities for growth. We grow and learn most when we embrace the "gray areas" of life, where there is room for flexibility and exploration.

While there are definitely times when dualistic thinking can be helpful, more often than not, it only serves to amplify situations that don't need to be amplified. So, how do we break free from this cycle? The answer is simple: shift your mindset.

The first step is to recognize when you're falling into dualistic thinking. You might catch yourself playing out "if-then" scenarios—"If I don't do this, then that will happen." When this occurs, take a moment to pause. Remind yourself that dualities are learned habits, and like any habit, they can be broken. Simply labeling the duality when you notice it can help you detach from it. You might say, "This is a duality, and I don't need to focus on it right now." With practice, you'll find it easier to catch these moments before they take over your thoughts. You'll begin to feel lighter, more free, and more open to new possibilities.

Over time, as you get better at identifying dualities in your thinking, you'll notice a shift in your mindset. You'll feel less stressed and more confident in your decision-making, which will make life feel smoother and more enjoyable. It's a simple but powerful change that has the potential to improve your overall well-being.

As you start eliminating dualities from your life, you'll likely see some amazing benefits: better sleep, healthier habits, less stress, and a greater sense of peace. By identifying dualities, you're actively shaping your inner world to be more in tune with who you truly are, allowing you to move through life with ease and clarity.

Once you experience the positive shift that comes from releasing these unnecessary mental distractions, it will become second nature. You'll catch yourself before the dualities even take hold, and your life will feel less stressful, more open, and more aligned with your true self. So, why wait? Start now. The next time you notice yourself stuck in an either-or moment, pause and label it: "This is a duality." Just that simple awareness is often enough to bring you back to center—where peace lives.

Day 18.

Let the Old Break

"Sometimes the breaking is the beginning—not the end."

Sometimes, we have to let the old crumble to make room for something new. And while this may seem like a choice, in many cases, it's not. It's simply how life works. Letting the old break is how we clear the way for better things to come along.

Have you ever watched an old town become new again? Or seen a building revitalized with a fresh coat of paint, breathing new life into its weathered facade? There's something captivating about watching the old transform into the new. The process of change, the phoenix-like rebirth, is often more exciting than creating from scratch.

We typically don't think about making repairs or upgrades until something breaks—and that's completely normal. Yet, when all is said and done, how often do we end up with something better than what we had before? It's as though, in the process of fixing what's broken, we find a newer, improved version of the original.

Letting the old break can be difficult, though, especially when we have attachments to the past. Have you ever asked yourself, "How long am I going to keep fixing this before I finally replace it?" Or "When am I going to stop putting up with this?" These attachments, while familiar and comforting, can often become unhealthy, especially when they drain our energy or hold us back from moving forward. It's human nature to resist change, to hold on to what feels comfortable, even when it no longer serves us. Acknowledging this can make it easier to let go of the past and make room for what's next.

The old saying, "Out with the old, in with the new," is true, but it's not just about replacing physical items—it's about emotional clutter too. Often, the things we need to let go of aren't objects at all—they're thought patterns or past memories. Do you have thoughts that keep looping, memories of hurt or regret, filled with "If I had only's"? You're not alone —and the good news is, you don't have to hold onto them.

Just like replacing worn-out furniture, sometimes we need to change the way we think. Outdated beliefs or unproductive thought patterns can weigh us down just as much as a broken appliance. If a thought or belief is holding you back, consider why it's still there—and if it's time to let it go.

Stuck patterns show up everywhere—not just in our personal lives, but also in our communities and the world at large. We see them in outdated media narratives, workplace conflicts, politics, and obsolete opinions. But here's the truth: all things heal in time, and old systems must often break in order to make way for something new and better to emerge. This is simply how life works. So, when something begins to fall apart, try not to resist it. That space is often where new and exciting opportunities begin to take shape.

How do we begin to let the old break? The first step is simply to acknowledge that it's time. You might feel it in your gut when something no longer fits, when it's holding you back or draining your energy. Start by identifying those areas where you've been resisting change—whether it's a relationship, a habit, a belief, or even a physical object. Reflect on what's holding you back, and ask yourself if it's truly serving you anymore. If the answer is no, that may be your sign to begin letting it go.

Once you recognize it, allow yourself to release the attachment. This doesn't mean you have to do it all at once. Start small, take baby steps, and trust that each time you let go, you're creating space for something new and better. Over time, letting go becomes easier, and you begin to see the beauty in the breaking.

Whether it's a car that constantly needs repairs or a habit that's holding you back, it's time to let go. Make room for something better. Think of the butterfly: it couldn't spread its wings until the caterpillar's body was left behind. What will you become when you finally let go of the old? What will you make room for in your life? Sit with these questions—and when you're ready, let go of what no longer serves you. Notice how it frees you. Then, watch what begins to grow in the space you've made. What you find may surprise you.

Day 19.

Get Out of Your Way

"The moment you stop seeking validation from others, you begin clearing the path to your own happiness."

"Do you think I should quit my job?"

"What do you think about this shirt?"

"Do you think I should sell my house?"

"What do you think about him/her?"

Have you ever asked anyone these questions? Or perhaps a version of them? I'll admit, I've asked similar questions before. Here are some responses I might give:

"Do *you* think you should quit your job?"

"I don't have to wear the shirt, *you* do. What do *you* think about it?"

"Do *you* want to live somewhere else?"

"It doesn't matter what I think about him/her. What do *you* think?"

Of course, there are times when we genuinely benefit from others' opinions, but too often, we find ourselves relying on their reassurances—becoming dependent on them—when, in reality, we should be looking to ourselves for answers. The truth is that the opinions of others rarely help us as much as we think they do, yet we seek them out anyway. We make our happiness conditional on what others think—which is like saying, "I'll be happy if they give me permission to be happy." When we do this, we're standing in our own way—and it's time to move over.

And what exactly are we standing in the way of?

Our happiness, our joy, and our peace.

No one else will ever fully understand what it's like to walk in your shoes. No one's opinion about your happiness truly matters, because they aren't the ones who get to live your life. Take a moment to really absorb that. *No one.* No one will ever know what you feel, think, or desire. That's why only you can choose what's right and best for you.

When we ask for opinions unnecessarily, we're placing our happiness in the hands of others. The trouble is, they often don't put the same thought into their answers as we do into our questions. Not only is this a type of codependence, but it's also unnecessary—and it can lead us down paths we never intended to take. We need to make sure we're the ones steering the ship, not someone else.

When you find yourself seeking approval, remember: you're standing in the way of the natural flow of your life. To move out of your own way, stop needing or asking for feedback. Outside opinions only weigh us down by influencing how we feel. And when all is said and done, it's just not worth it. In the long run, we always get where we're going, so why take pit stops or detours based on someone else's input?

Imagine this: Each path you take is like a journey in a board game. You place your marker on "GO" and roll the dice. As you make your way around the board, you know your goal is to reach the finish line—your happiness—and the journey itself is the fun along the way. Would you let someone else take your turn? Would you allow them to move your marker and decide where you land, even though they have their own game to play? Maybe you'd let them, but it's unlikely. Doesn't that take the fun out of it?

Do yourself a favor and play your own turn.

Free yourself from the burden of seeking outside opinions. Get out of your way, and let life flow toward you.

Now, go ahead and move—it's your turn to play.

Day 20.

Remember Your Forgotten

"The things you loved aren't gone. You just forgot they were there."

It's never too late to remember your forgotten. *Your* forgotten—not you're (as in *you are*) forgotten—your forgotten, as in, your forgotten stuff. Your forgotten what? Your forgotten passions.

What happened to the things you used to do for fun? Surely, at some point, you had fun. Hobbies? Passions? Where are they now? Isn't it time to bring them back out—or perhaps find new ones? Are they hiding in the closet, under the bed, tucked away in storage somewhere—or are they just buried in your mind?

While it's not advisable to live in the past, rekindling activities that once filled you with joy can often be one of the quickest ways to bring bliss back into your life. Reconnecting with those forgotten passions can reignite a spark that's been dormant for too long.

Take a moment to think about the things you once loved to do. What are they? Where are they now?

Make a list of things you used to do for fun—things that made you smile because you've experienced them before. Treat it like a grocery list, leaving room to check off things you'd like to do again. This way, you'll have a go-to list of pleasures that are sure to bring a sense of joy and rejuvenate your spirit.

Do you remember looking forward to free time? *Me* time? If you still get to enjoy me time, that's fantastic! But what about more? When was the last time you scheduled precious reunion time with your forgotten passions? Life has a way of filling up our calendars, but there's always room for what truly brings us joy.

Exploring new avenues of joy is always a great idea, too. But don't forget about the passions you once loved. They're like an old recipe—comforting, familiar, and always bringing you back to who you were.

As you spend time reflecting on your forgotten, remember: the things you loved aren't gone. You just forgot they were there. It's time to give them space to resurface. When you welcome back these forgotten parts of yourself, you're not just reconnecting with activities—you're reconnecting with what makes you feel alive.

Sometimes, the act of rediscovering old passions can lead to new insights about who you are now. Maybe the things you once loved no longer resonate with you in the same way, and that's okay. But in rediscovering what used to light you up, you may find new paths that speak to the person you've become. Remembering your forgotten passions isn't about chasing the past—it's about letting those sparks evolve with you, adding meaning to who you are now.

So, let the reunion begin. Isn't it time to remember?

Day 21.

Charge Yourself

"Rest isn't a luxury—it's the way back to yourself."

Technology has transformed the way we live—just look at electric cars. When they run low on energy, we don't race to a gas station. We plug in and recharge—easily, effortlessly. The same goes for our cell phones, laptops, tablets, digital music players, e-readers, hearing aids, and countless other smart devices. Keeping the things we rely on up and running has never been easier—all it takes is a quick charge, and everything is good to go.

With all the plugging and charging we do for our devices, it's worth asking: Are we doing the same for ourselves? When was the last time you rested enough to truly feel your best? In other words, when was the last time you charged *yourself*?

If you're like most of us, you get just enough sleep each night to wake up and tackle another round of daily routines. But what does "enough" sleep really mean? Personally, I struggle with being a night owl, often cutting my sleep short by an hour or two to fit in more. How about you?

Maybe once a year, we take a vacation to recharge. And if we're lucky, that vacation is actually relaxing. But why do vacations feel so refreshing? It's because they offer a break from our usual routines, replacing stress with moments of ease or carefree distraction. It feels so good because, let's face it—our everyday lives can be draining. We all need time to recharge. And honestly, hallway outlets don't exactly inspire joy. So why not recharge by the ocean, under the sun, or somewhere that actually feels like rest?

But what if you didn't have to wait for a vacation to feel rested, emotionally reset, and mentally free? The good news is —you don't! We can recharge more efficiently without leaving the comfort of our homes, if we simply know how. It's a two-step process: giving your body the rest it needs and eliminating unnecessary energy drains.

First, let's talk about sleep. We can't function at our best if we aren't getting the sleep our bodies need. Our mental health, physical health, and overall quality of life will suffer if we don't prioritize rest. Understand this, and make it a point to receive the proper amount of sleep.

So, how much sleep is enough? It varies for everyone. Most people need 7-9 hours of sleep to feel rested, but your body will tell you exactly what it needs. Pay attention to your own signs of fatigue and adjust accordingly. For some, 8 hours might feel like the magic number, while others may need more or less. The key is listening to your body and ensuring you're getting enough to feel your best.

To help improve your sleep, try a few of these tips:

1. **Limit Caffeine and Alcohol**
   Avoid caffeine in the evening, and remember—while alcohol can make you drowsy, it also disrupts sleep cycles.

2. **Know Your Sleep Needs**
   Most people need 7–9 hours—experiment and find what feels right.

3. **Have a Comfortable Sleep Environment**
   Keep your space dark, quiet, and cool. Invest in a good mattress and comfy bedding.

4. **Manage Stress and Anxiety**
   Try journaling, deep breathing, or even an evening walk. Avoid screens and late-night stressors.

5. **Exercise Regularly**
   Regular exercise helps with rest, but don't work out too close to bedtime.

While sleep is essential, it's equally important to eliminate the things that drain our energy during the day. For example, we often think that zoning out in front of a screen helps us recharge—but it doesn't. Our minds and bodies remain engaged with whatever we focus on. Whether we're watching an action-packed movie or a horror film, our emotions are activated, and we absorb whatever energy is being projected. Even background noise from TV shows, books, or conversations can affect our state of mind. If it's not relaxing or calming, it can interfere with your rest and should be avoided before bed.

Your mind and body need daily rest and recharging more than any device you own. You can't thrive without it. As you work toward becoming the best version of yourself, it's essential to make time for self-care and recharging. Start by incorporating a few of these tips, and notice how you feel tomorrow. The benefits come quickly—and once you feel the difference, you won't want to go back to running on empty.

Day 22.

Pay Attention to What Resonates

"When something resonates, follow it. That's how you build a life you actually love."

Ever felt goosebumps from a song, a phrase, or even a smell? That reaction isn't random—it's a signal. It's your inner compass pointing toward something meaningful. When a moment grabs your attention, it's worth noticing—because moving in that direction is how you build a life you actually love.

For example, if we're passionate about cooking, aren't we naturally drawn to fancy kitchen gadgets? Or if we love working with our hands, do we not find ourselves attracted to tools and hardware? When we pay attention to what resonates with us and move in that direction, we open ourselves up to a happier, more fulfilling life—one filled with things that bring joy and make us smile.

Why do some experiences resonate and others don't? Because not everything is meant for us—and that's okay. Our bodies often know before our minds do; they're possibly our most reliable messenger. When we quiet our rational minds for just a moment and tune into the impulses of our hearts, we usually know what to do. Like a compass pointing north, our intuition guides us toward what feels right. But do we allow ourselves to follow that pull, to move in the direction that brings us joy—even if just for a moment? Some of us do, but many of us don't.

Here are a few reasons why it's important to pay attention to what resonates with us:

- **Boosts Fulfillment**
  Bringing what we love into our lives—people, passions, or places—connects us to what matters and reminds us that joy isn't a luxury—it's a sign we're in harmony.

- **Strengthens Decision-Making**
  Resonance acts like an inner compass. Whether it's career shifts or relationship choices, the things that "just feel right" usually are.

- **Aligns You With Your Values**
  When you follow what resonates, your actions begin to reflect your true self. That alignment creates peace, clarity, and confidence.

- **Increases Self-Awareness**
  What energizes or drains you is a message. The more you notice, the more you understand yourself—and the easier it becomes to live intentionally.

So, how do we begin paying attention to what resonates? One simple method is to practice mindfulness. Be present and notice what's around you—tune in to what grabs your attention. Mindfulness means fully engaging with the moment. Are you aware when something stands out to you? Maybe you hear a catchy melody and find yourself drawn to it, or you smell the aroma of freshly baked goods that makes you stop and take a deep breath. This awareness helps bring the things we love into focus, gently guiding us toward what we truly desire.

Another way we can recognize what resonates is by learning to pay attention to our emotions. Do you find yourself energized by the thought of reading a book or going for a walk? Perhaps the idea of cleaning your home is enough to make you move. That burst of energy is a key indicator that it's something you may want to pursue. Likewise, a drop in energy may be a sign to avoid certain people or tasks. It's all about listening to your body and moving toward what's best for you.

Another powerful clue is noticing where you feel the least resistance. Have you ever felt how certain activities or people make you feel lighter, while others weigh you down? This can be a subtle but important signal. Life doesn't always need to feel like an uphill battle—when we pay attention to what flows effortlessly, we are often closer to aligning with our true path. So, next time you feel drained or energized by a task, take a moment to pause and assess where your energy is naturally flowing.

Journaling can be a helpful way to reflect on what lifts your energy—and what brings you down. When you notice things that resonate with you, ask yourself questions like, "Why did this catch my attention? Why did this make me happy?" or "Why didn't I enjoy this as much as I thought I would?"

Over time, you'll recognize patterns in what you truly desire, gaining a deeper understanding of what appeals to you. As your awareness grows, you'll find yourself moving more mindfully through life, embracing opportunities to experience joy and satisfaction whenever possible.

When you pay attention to what resonates, life becomes less about getting through the day and more about living it. You fill your hours with people, projects, and places that nourish your soul. Start noticing. Follow the spark. Let resonance be your roadmap—and watch how your life begins to light up from the inside out.

Day 23.

Mind Your Words

"The voice that speaks loudest in your life is the one you hear inside. Make sure it's saying the right things."

Sticks and stones can break your bones, but words will never hurt you.

Right?

Wrong.

Words do hurt—and they shape us.

Even if we train ourselves to have thick skin or strong egos, words still have an impact. They affect us because words reach our emotions in ways actions sometimes can't. This is why affirmations work—when we hear something often enough, we start to believe it. Anyone who uses positive affirmations to guide their thoughts and behaviors knows this firsthand. Similarly, anyone who's been on the receiving end of negative or demeaning language understands just how deeply insults and put-downs can hurt.

Have you ever spent a lot of time around someone whose negativity or attitude drained you? Many of us have—and some of us still do.

Maybe you've been in the middle of a conversation, listening to someone complain about everything under the sun, and thought, "I can't be around this person anymore," or "I'm spending too much time around this person." If that moment hasn't happened, is there someone in your life you should be saying this about?

If you're constantly around someone who uses negative language or brings down your energy, have you paused to notice how it's affecting you? Try stepping back for a while and see if your mood shifts. It can be life-changing—removing yourself from negativity and making space for positive energy to flow in. Words affect us—mentally, emotionally, even physically. That's why it's so important to recognize their impact and make changes when needed.

Negativity doesn't just stay with us—it lingers. The words others use often create a mental echo, replaying in our minds long after the conversation ends. That echo can cloud our mental clarity, chip away at our confidence, and distort how we see ourselves. In contrast, when we surround ourselves with positive, affirming language, we create an environment of growth and possibility. Those words uplift and encourage, helping us move forward instead of keeping us stuck.

And while the words of others matter, it's the ones we whisper to ourselves that can do the deepest damage.

Our own self-talk is powerful—sometimes more so than anything spoken aloud. We can avoid certain people or limit our exposure to external negativity, but our internal voice travels with us wherever we go. If that voice is overly critical or harsh, it becomes a constant source of pressure and pain. The good news—you can change the script.

Start replacing harsh inner language with affirmations that reflect your worth and potential. You don't need to be perfect—you just need to be kind to yourself. Try something like, "I'm doing the best I can," or "I deserve happiness." The more you practice, the more positive self-talk becomes second nature—reshaping how you feel about yourself and your place in the world. Over time, those repeated, gentle words become your beliefs.

We often hear about the benefits of positive language, but we don't talk enough about how damaging negative words can be. Start paying attention to the language you use. If you catch yourself saying something demeaning—about yourself or others—pause. Rephrase it, or say nothing at all. That one small decision could change your entire day.

Words have the power to create the reality we live in. When we use language that uplifts, inspires, and supports, we begin to experience a life that reflects those same qualities. On the other hand, when we choose words that tear down or limit us, we create a world that does the same. Speak gently. Speak with kindness.

And remember: while sticks and stones may break bones, the wrong words will always leave a mark. Speak gently—especially to yourself—and you'll begin to notice your entire world softening in return.

Day 24.

It's Never Going to Be Easy

"The road isn't meant to be easy—it's meant to reveal who you really are."

It's never going to be easy.

Life, that is—it's never going to be easy.

But don't let that discourage you. In fact, the further we go on our journey, the greater the challenges we face. That's not to say we'll eventually face challenges we can't handle. On the contrary, as we progress, we get better at overcoming obstacles. The difficulty increases, but so does our ability to navigate it. This is by design: life's challenges evolve to match our growing strength, so, yes, it's never going to be easy—but we get pretty good at handling it, and even start to enjoy the ride.

Think about when you were young. First grade was hard, but it was fun. It was hard because everything was new—

learning letters and numbers, developing social skills, practicing independence. Those challenges brought happiness because, as kids, we instinctively knew how to embrace life, even when it was demanding. As you grew, third grade became harder. Fifth grade? Even harder. By the time you hit twelfth grade, it was much tougher—but only in comparison to where you started. The difference wasn't that it became impossible—it's that, as you moved through school, you were naturally prepared for more advanced subjects and greater responsibility. Each year, the difficulty level increased, but it was always manageable because you had built up the skills to handle it.

Personal development works the same way. You begin with simple concepts: letting go of limiting beliefs, learning to manage reactions, living in the moment. As you grow, you tackle deeper challenges, like understanding world peace or learning how to coexist with almost anyone. Steady progress is completely normal—there's no need to rush. Just like in school, you can't learn advanced concepts until you master the basics. Each new step will bring its own set of challenges, but those challenges will always be rewarding. As you shed old habits and restrictive routines, you make room for new opportunities to grow and succeed. This is how we evolve—one step at a time, replacing outdated beliefs with ideas that serve us better.

It's easy to look at challenges and think they'll never end or that we'll never be "good enough" to handle them. But the truth is, the longer we continue on this journey of growth, the more we realize that every challenge, no matter how tough, carries within it the seeds of opportunity. It's often in the hardest moments that we learn the most about ourselves. We uncover hidden strengths, discover new ways of thinking, and push past limits we once thought impossible.

These experiences aren't just obstacles to overcome—they're the building blocks of who we are becoming.

Eventually, we begin to look at difficulties not as setbacks, but as stepping stones.

Pointing out that life isn't going to be easy, isn't meant to discourage you—it's simply something to keep in mind as you move forward. Every personal victory paves the way for bigger accomplishments. If you haven't yet experienced the relief that comes when lifelong struggles fade away, you will—because, if you do the work, it's coming. Remember that everything you do to improve yourself is progress, even if it doesn't always feel easy. The road may be tough, but it will always be rewarding.

The key to navigating these challenges is perseverance. It's not about avoiding the difficulties, but learning to push through them with resilience. We sometimes fall into the trap of thinking everything should be smooth sailing.

But it's the rough waters that teach us how to steer the ship.

The more we face our struggles head-on, the more we realize that, although life's challenges will never go away, we've developed the tools to not just survive them, but thrive in spite of them. This is where growth happens—when we keep going, even when the climb feels steep.

When life becomes overwhelming, remember: you control your perspective. Choose happiness, and you'll look back with fondness, grateful for both the journey and the growth it brought. Don't shy away from the hard moments— they're what shape you. You were meant to find joy in who you are and all that life has to offer. If that weren't true, you wouldn't be here.

One of the most powerful things you can do in difficult times is to remember why you started. When the path gets steep, it's easy to lose sight of the bigger picture. But every challenge you face is a chance to become more of who you're meant to be. The moments that stretch you the most often arrive just before major change happens.

Keep your eyes on the prize: the version of yourself that emerges from this—stronger, wiser, and more fully alive.

Eventually, you'll see that the challenge wasn't in your way—it was the way.

Day 25.

What's in a Name?

*"A name is not your identity—it's the starting point.
Discover where it leads."*

Who are you? When you meet someone new, what do you say? Do you share your name? Great—so, what name do you give them?

Chances are, you're repeating the name you were given at birth. And that's fine. But is it the full truth of who you are?

A name is just a label—given to you by one or two people, based on what was meaningful to them at the time. Over the years, you've added your own meanings to it—based on what you do, how you see yourself, or how you've been seen by others: *I am good at my job, I am not good at my job, I am religious, I am funny, I am shy, I am conservative, I am liberal, I am _____ (state your name).* But if you stripped away your name, who would you say you are? You might say, *I am a teacher, I am a parent,* or *I am a friend.* Society often encourages us to define ourselves by our roles or what we do, but who are we, really?

The truth is, you are far more than just a name or a title. If that's all there was to you, you wouldn't be searching for answers; you'd simply state your name and be done with it. You are a powerful, creative individual—constantly evolving. Defining yourself by a single label is one of the greatest limitations you can place on your growth. The goal is self-realization: to understand that you are more than the labels you've carried and that you are capable of becoming whoever you want to be. So, who are you really, and how can you begin to see yourself as the ever-expanding, limitless person that you are?

If your name doesn't instantly spark feelings of self-love, joy, peace, and appreciation for life, something might need to shift. When was the last time you had a conversation with yourself? Have you ever? Have you told yourself that you are so much more than that shy, uncertain child who was too nervous to speak up in school? Have you forgiven yourself for the times you felt insecure? Have you acknowledged that you're allowed to make mistakes and grow—and reminded yourself that none of it defines who you are today? It might sound strange, but try making a habit of having conversations with yourself. Don't worry if you get a few strange looks sitting in traffic—it's bound to happen.

The way we see ourselves sets the tone for how others see us. If we're hard on ourselves, we're likely to see that reflected back when we interact with others. But if we walk with courage and confidence, others will pick up on that, too. What we think about ourselves—our names, our identities— directly shapes how we experience the world around us. When we assign positive, self-loving qualities to our lives, we attract the same energy back from the world. After all, isn't that how you'd like to be treated?

I remember a time when my friend struggled with her own name—both literally and figuratively. Growing up, she never felt comfortable with the assumptions tied to it. People would say things like, "You're just like your father," or "You should be more like your brother." These comparisons were tied to traits that didn't feel like her at all. It was as if her name came with a script she had no interest in following.

Eventually, she began to look beneath those surface-level labels and associations. She realized she was more than her family's daughter or the assumptions others made about her. She had the power to define herself and embrace a name that felt more aligned with who she was becoming. That shift gave her the strength to forge her own path. She went to school, built a career beyond what anyone expected —and today she's truly happy with the life she's created.

On a personal note, I once took a long look in the mirror and asked myself who I really was—beyond the roles and expectations placed upon me. I wasn't just the "'nice guy'" or the one you "'called when you needed something,'" nor was I the person I believed I had to be. I wasn't defined by my achievements or failures. I was capable of growth and of shifting how I viewed myself. That conversation wasn't easy, but it was necessary. It's what led to the creation of this book. It's when we have the courage to redefine the meaning of our names and embrace the evolving version of who we are that true transformation begins. Sometimes, we have to ask hard questions before we find the answers we're looking for.

It's incredibly freeing to realize that your name—your identity—isn't set in stone. Just because you were known as one thing in the past doesn't mean you have to stay there. You can always shift your perspective, change your approach, and, most importantly, embrace the limitless potential that lies within you. Each day is a chance to redefine yourself—whether in small moments or in the big choices you make. The labels you carry are yours to reshape, and in doing so, you can move closer to the version of yourself you truly want to be.

If you don't know yourself, it's unlikely anyone else will either. If you don't like the name you've been given—or the baggage it carries—change it. After all, what's in a name? It's just a word, shaped by the meanings you assign to it. Remember, you are a powerful, creative individual. Isn't it time you tried that label on for size?

Day 26.

The Power of Gratitude

"Gratitude doesn't ignore the dark—it keeps the light on, so you can find your way through."

Be grateful for everything. This simple act has been echoed through spiritual and religious traditions for centuries —and for good reason. Gratitude helps us focus on what we have rather than what we lack, and that shift alone can change everything. It improves our mental and emotional health, reduces stress, and strengthens our relationships. It builds resilience, nurtures contentment, and makes joy easier to access. Gratitude helps us slow down, savor small moments, and live more fully in the present. At its core, it's not just a feel-good habit—it's a foundation for personal growth and a more fulfilling life.

I remember a time when everything felt heavy—stress at work, personal losses, and a deep sense of isolation weighed me down. Everything seemed off, like life was testing me from every angle. But then, I paused. I made a list of the things I was still grateful for—my kids, my life experiences, even the small wins—and something shifted. That quiet moment of reflection didn't fix everything, but it helped me breathe again. Gratitude gave me a new lens. It didn't erase the hard stuff, but it reminded me there was still light—and that was enough to begin a new path toward peace of mind and happiness.

To live well—especially when things are hard—we need to practice gratitude regularly. The following are simple ways to bring more gratitude into your daily rhythm. They're not complicated, but when practiced consistently, they can gently reshape how you experience the world around you.

1. **Have an Attitude of Gratitude**
   Pause throughout your day to give thanks. Whether you're working, having a meal, or taking a walk, notice what brings you joy—and take a moment to appreciate it.

2. **Use Gratitude Reminders**
   Place sticky notes, set gentle phone alerts, or surround yourself with objects that prompt you to reflect. A favorite photo, a simple word, or a meaningful quote can bring you back to center.

3. **Reframe Negative Thoughts**
   When something goes wrong, challenge yourself to shift the focus. What did you learn? What still went

right? Gratitude isn't about ignoring pain—it's about seeing the whole picture.

4. **Keep a Gratitude Journal**
   Write down a few things you're grateful for each day. It doesn't have to be deep or detailed. Over time, this simple habit trains your mind to seek out what's good.

5. **Give Gratitude Freely**
   Tell someone how they've made your life better. A text, a note, or a heartfelt moment can go a long way—for them and for you.

6. **Do Something That Fills You With Gratitude**
   Make space for the little things that light you up— reading a book, moving your body, sitting in stillness. Living with gratitude isn't just about what you think; it's about what you choose to do.

It's widely accepted that life gets better when we cultivate an attitude of gratitude. Our relationships deepen, our mental and physical health strengthen, and we feel more content walking in our own shoes. By focusing on the good that's already present, we adopt a mindset of appreciation that carries over into other areas of our lives. When practiced regularly, gratitude shifts our perspective—making it easier to experience joy, find meaning, and stay grounded in a more positive state. Gratitude helps us embrace the present moment, appreciate the people and experiences that enrich our lives, and leads us toward a more meaningful and rewarding existence.

Practicing gratitude when life is going well is one thing. But when everything feels like it's falling apart—that's when the rubber hits the road, and the practice becomes something even more important.

Over time, I've learned that gratitude isn't just a response to joy—it's a tool for clearing out the clutter and making room for happiness to enter (or re-enter) your life. In the hardest moments, it doesn't have to be a big revelation. Sometimes, it's just a breath. A simple reminder that even now, there's still something good: the warmth of sunlight, the sound of a loved one's voice, the comfort of simply making it through the day.

Gratitude in hard times doesn't deny the pain—it gives us something solid to hold onto. It becomes a quiet strength. A soft anchor when everything else feels unsteady.

Start weaving gratitude into your daily life. It's not just about feeling good in the moment—it's about opening yourself up to more joy, more connection, and a deeper understanding of the process of life. Over time, this simple practice can shift the way you see the world and the way you see yourself. And as you start to live with more gratitude, you may just find that the path forward feels a little lighter, a little clearer, and a whole lot easier to walk.

Day 27.

Listen

"The answer to everything is already inside you. But the question is—do you listen?"

Do you listen?

Listen to what?

To your own inner voice—it's called intuition.

When you were growing up, you might have called it your conscience, or perhaps your "gut," as in, "trust your gut" or "gut instinct." The name doesn't matter. What's important is recognizing and using this powerful tool. You came into this world already equipped with it—your very own on-board guidance system. So why not use it?

What exactly is intuition? It's that voice inside that tells you to think twice before speeding up, reminds you of a loved one's birthday, or nudges you to reach out to a friend. It's the voice that tells you when to pick up the phone, buy extra milk, or take an alternate route to avoid traffic. Sometimes, it even saves lives with advice like, "don't go down that street," or "make sure to lock the door." Intuition is your inner guiding light, steering you in the right direction. You could think of it as your personal radar—or maybe even an extension of your own guardian angel.

Let's break it down: "tuit" means to know or understand, and "in" means inner or inside. So, **in-tuit-ion** literally means inner knowing, or the knowing that comes from within you.

It's true what they say: the answer to everything is already inside you. But the question is—do you listen? Do you tap into this "intuition," this sixth sense, that so many people talk about? If you haven't been listening, rest assured—it's there, waiting for you to notice and put it to use.

Many people spend years—even a lifetime—honing their intuition. For beginners, the first step is simply choosing to tune in. Start by paying attention to your own inner guidance throughout the day. Let it inform your small choices —when to reach out to someone, when to pause, where to go. The more you ask, the more it answers. And if you get it wrong now and then, don't stress—it just means you're still learning how to listen.

Intuition doesn't always speak in words—it could be a feeling, an impulse, a hesitation, a chill on your skin, or the sudden urge to look in a different direction. It's about learning to decipher the language of intuition and recognizing its signals. What does caution feel like? What does a confirmation feel like? Practice being mindful of your feelings —over time, you'll get the hang of it.

Listening to your body is a great way to sharpen your intuitive skills. It's amazing how much you already know— even if you've forgotten, it's still there.

You were born knowing how to listen to yourself. Nobody had to tell you to smile back when your parents smiled at you or to laugh when they made you feel safe. No one had to explain why a stranger's face frightened you or why you missed the comfort of being held when you were learning to sleep on your own. Intuition was the answer to all of those questions. It's our natural ability to discern what's good for us and what's not. You could call it a "survival instinct," and you'd be right.

We were all born with intuition. But over time, life speeds up, and outside voices grow louder. We let other people tell us what to do, or we fall into the habit of living on autopilot, making decisions without thinking. When we just go through the motions, we stop listening to our hearts. By reconnecting with our intuition, we reignite the same survival mechanisms that guided us as babies. The system that knew how to trust and find comfort in our parents is still with us— it's built into our biology, designed to keep us safe, and always guiding us toward what's best.

Sometimes, we don't listen to our intuition because we doubt ourselves or feel too much pressure from the outside world. But intuition doesn't need validation from others—it's personal, internal, and aligned with who you are at your core. The more you listen, the more you'll realize that you don't need to look for answers outside of yourself. You are your best guide.

When we use our intuition, we're navigating life more mindfully—avoiding unnecessary struggles, making healthier decisions, and choosing the paths that feel most aligned with who we are. Intuition doesn't just guide us toward safer choices; it helps us experience more joy, peace, and fulfillment along the way.

Do you use your intuition? Do you listen to it enough? If the answer is no, consider this: sharpening your intuitive skills can add immeasurable value to your life. It's never too late to start—your intuition has been there all along, just waiting for you to notice it.

The answer has always been inside of you—start listening.

Day 28.

Trust

"Trust doesn't mean you won't be affected—it means you'll make it through, and no matter what happens, you know you always will."

There's no denying it: the world offers endless opportunities to find problems if we're looking for them. Every day, in every season, a few things are guaranteed—like the sun rising and taxes coming due. They're the constants we can set our watches to. And right alongside them? Triggers at work, stress about personal finances, global headlines, noisy neighbors, long lines, and traffic. These aren't things we enjoy —but we can't avoid them entirely.

The good news? You don't have to let them bother you. Learning how to stay grounded in the face of everyday stress is too important to put off. After all, unless you've signed up for a career in religious seclusion, you can't entirely escape the world's challenges. And for most of us, living apart from society isn't healthy, even if we could. So, how do we handle all this?

The key isn't to avoid these situations entirely (though that can help); it's to rise above what challenges you—and stop letting it bother you. And how do you do that? Simple: you trust. Trust in what, exactly? In yourself? In others?

No. Trust in the flow of the universe, in God, in a higher power—call it whatever you like. You're trusting that nothing stays the same forever. The sun will set as surely as it rises. Deadlines will come and go. Spring will fade into summer, and summer will blend into fall. Nothing remains frozen in time. This is what you need to believe in. And believing this will always carry you through life.

Stress, anxiety, and other negative emotions arise when we get trapped in the present moment—believing that what we're feeling will never end. We forget that life moves on. And when it does, we realize that endings often pass just as quickly as they arrived. Yes, actions have reactions, causes have effects. Our thoughts and words have consequences—good or bad—and shape our experiences. But no matter what happens, our current state won't last forever. Fully understanding this can alleviate much of the pain we feel in difficult moments. The key is remembering that everything is temporary. This simple awareness helps you rise above setbacks. And, eventually, you'll realize that setbacks won't bother you at all.

Here's a quick exercise: think of a stressful situation that caused you anxiety, fear, worry, or doubt. Don't relive it—

just recall it. For most of us, this won't be hard. Think of something you faced and overcame—whether it was the death of a loved one, a divorce, losing a job, or dealing with a financial crisis. The fact that you're reading this right now shows you made it through.

You might be thinking, "No, I wasn't alright. I didn't sleep, I ate too much, I drank too much, I smoked too much. I fought with my family. My blood pressure was through the roof." But guess what? You survived—and that means you're stronger than the worst thing that ever happened to you.

And maybe you're thinking, "Well, that's easy for you to say." And yes, it is. But consider this: during that time, what if you had trusted that you would make it through? What if you had known, deep down, that no matter what happened, your basic needs would be met, and eventually, you would sleep, breathe, and wake up again? How much of the torment you experienced could have been avoided? Probably a lot.

Now imagine that same situation again—and know: You didn't just survive—you learned something in the process. Maybe you learned resilience. Maybe you learned that you're stronger than you thought. Here's the thing: the more you practice trust, the more you'll realize you have the ability to weather any storm. The trust you build today will carry you through whatever challenges lie ahead.

Trust doesn't mean that nothing will ever affect you. It means you'll be alright—and that you have the inner strength to make it through, especially when that's hard to believe. Even the darkest tunnels have light at the end. Trust is a lifelong process, and it often means walking through the muck before you can master it.

Start now. When you're stuck in traffic, trust that it will eventually clear. When you're feeling stressed, trust that the day will get better. And when you're hangry, trust that food will soon be on its way. Trust that everything will be okay. Begin small, and let your trust build. Remember, you're doing this work for your greatest good—to live the best life possible, filled with peace and ease. Learning to trust the process of life will allow you to rise above most challenges and shield yourself from outside influences. It may be difficult at first, but with a little practice, it will become second nature. *Trust* that it will.

Day 29.

You Are Not a Victim

"The story isn't what happened to you—it's who you became because of it."

You are not a victim. It might not always feel that way —but it's the truth. Nothing happens to you. No matter how you feel or what you've been told, the world doesn't target you. You are not a victim, and the universe is not a bully.

Here's the truth: everything happens for us or through us; nothing happens to us. Every experience—everything we've done or will ever do—either benefits us or benefits others through us. This is a universal truth: all things provide opportunities for us to become better versions of ourselves. Let's explore the first way this truth shows up in life:

For Us

Every experience—whether good or bad—is ultimately for our benefit. When something is for you, it leads to positive growth in some way. When things go well, we can embrace them, repeat the experience, and invite more of that enjoyment into our lives. When things go wrong, we're given a chance to grow stronger, wiser, and better prepared for what comes next. Even the hardest moments build resilience and teach perspective.

Take something simple: missing a payment, forgetting an appointment, or arriving at the store and finding what you need is out of stock. These moments are frustrating—but they don't have to be. Each one has the power to nudge you toward something better—like increased awareness, stronger habits, or even a surprising alternative you wouldn't have considered otherwise.

They may feel inconvenient, but they don't have to defeat you—especially if you choose to take something from them. When you start looking at life through the lens of personal growth, even setbacks become opportunities. It's not about being perfect—it's about moving forward and making each moment count.

This shift in perspective changes everything. You stop seeing mistakes as failures—and start seeing them as fuel. Reflect on your own experiences—the good and the challenging—and chances are, you'll see how every one of them shaped you in some way. Growth doesn't always feel good in the moment, but it always serves us in the end.

Through Us

We are all conduits for good. Our actions and experiences can impact others in meaningful ways—if we allow them to. Each of us holds the power not only to shape our own lives, but to influence others through the choices we make every day.

Hold the door. Lend a hand. Leave a generous tip. These are small ways the universe works through you—and in return, you open yourself up to receive the same.

Has anyone ever helped you out? A kind glance that brightened your day? A break when you needed it? This is the universe working through someone else to assist you. It's a continuous flow of goodwill—giving and receiving—that we're all a part of. Offer your part with appreciation, grace, and ease, and watch how it flows back to you.

Didn't you grow up hearing, "It's better to give than to receive"? Sacred and secular teachings alike emphasize this. We repeat it because it reflects a truth we all feel—that giving is part of who we are, and it creates real, lasting impact. Try it and see.

But even with all this in mind, it's easy to slip back into the feeling that life is working against us. That's where the third truth comes in. Understanding that *life happens for us and through* us brings clarity—but to truly shift our mindset, we also have to let go of the idea that anything ever happens to us.

Not to Us

When things go wrong, it can feel like life is working against us. But that mindset keeps us stuck. The truth is, nothing is happening to us—it's just happening. And how we interpret it is everything.

Believing that "it's just one thing after another" or "I knew this good luck couldn't last" keeps you locked in a victim mentality. It's not just false—it's dangerous, because it keeps you from growing. When we realize that nothing happens to us, we shed the fear of living and allow life's benefits to flow to us. And when we stop believing the world is against us, the weight of stress and anxiety begins to lift.

Believing that everything happens to you is a choice—and it's not a healthy one. You have to let go of it. The sooner you do, the sooner you open yourself up to a better life.

It's time to move on from the old way of thinking—the one that says life is against you. What if that was never true? What if nothing was ever working against you—but always working with you? How different might your daily challenges feel? How many hard moments could've turned out differently? How many obstacles might've been easier to handle, simply by adjusting your perspective?

That's the shift—from letting life happen to you, to trusting the process, and noticing how the world responds. When your perspective changes, life doesn't just feel different —it becomes different.

You begin to notice the pauses between moments. You stop needing everything to make sense right away.

Opportunities appear. Peace finds its way in. And things begin to move in your favor.

Because life happens for you. Life happens through you. Never to you.

And in that shift, you begin to come home to yourself.

Day 30.

Keep Climbing

"It's not just about reaching the top—it's about who we become on the way up."

Have you ever walked away from something you once felt committed to? Maybe it was a goal, a relationship, a job, or even a promise you made to yourself. Most of us have faced that moment—when the excitement fades, the obstacles start to build, or the finish line feels too far away.

Sometimes, walking away is the right move. It frees us. But that's not what we're talking about here. This is about the times we've stepped away—not because something was wrong, but because it got hard. We've all been there. And if we've done it more than once, it doesn't mean we're failures—it means we're human.

What matters is noticing the pattern: what causes us to step away—and when does it tend to happen?

Sometimes we move on because it's the healthiest choice. But we have to be honest about what's driving that decision. Are we walking away because it no longer fits—or because it became uncomfortable?

Years ago, I was in a career I truly loved—something that felt like a great fit for who I was. But I left it, chasing what I thought were greener pastures. I convinced myself I would find something better—more peace in my life, more happiness. What I found instead was a hard truth: greener pastures don't always exist. Sometimes we leave something meaningful not because it's wrong, but because we're restless.

That lesson stayed with me. Later, when Covid hit, my business took a major hit—every path forward felt like a quick route to a long, slow decline. Delays. Doubt. Exhaustion. I wondered if I had what it took to persevere.

But this time, I kept going. I remembered what it felt like to quit too soon—how long it took to sit with that regret. Even though it felt heavy, I stayed with it. Not from pride or pressure. But because I sensed there was still something meaningful there—and that I wasn't done yet. That business became more than a goal—it became a mirror. A place that showed me what I was capable of, and how much growth is possible when you stay with something through the hard parts.

The climb changes us. It's not just about reaching the top—it's about who we become on the way up.

When the trail gets rocky, when the end feels far off, or when doubt creeps in—that's when we remind ourselves to keep climbing. Pushing forward isn't about pretending we're not tired. It's about noticing those feelings—but not letting them steer your decisions. No one reaches the top without struggle. The ones who make it are the ones who keep going— one step, one breath at a time.

Perseverance changes us. Think back to a time when you gave up on something you now wish you'd finished. What did that experience teach you? Maybe it revealed how deeply you actually cared—or how quickly you walked away before giving it a real chance. Either way, that lesson can become fuel for your next effort.

We all need encouragement—a nudge to push on. So pause and remind yourself: keep climbing. You're not just making changes. You're becoming someone new. The fact that you're reading this proves you're committed to something better. And that's worth being proud of!

The road you're on may be hard—but it's also a testament to your strength and your commitment to growth. Don't expect it to be easy. Before you choose to walk away from a commitment, simply ask yourself: does this decision reflect who I'm becoming—or who I'm afraid to be?

If the answer is rooted in truth, follow it. But if it's rooted in fear, stay the course. Just because something feels uncomfortable doesn't mean it's the wrong path. Staying firm in what matters most is always the best way forward.

Here's what I know: no one will ever support you more, believe in you more deeply, or stay as committed to your journey as you will. So when things get tough, and that voice whispers, "Maybe it's time to quit," gently answer back: "not yet." Keep climbing.

The goal is just as beautiful as you imagine—and the view from the top will make every step worth it. Not just for what you'll see, but for who you'll become along the way. Wherever you are right now, hold onto this: keep climbing. And when you reach the top, you'll be glad you didn't stop.

Day 31.

Advice to End a Vice

"You might love the habit, but you love yourself more."

A vice is a bad habit—something that chips away at your time, energy, or well-being. Some are small, like overspending or constantly checking your phone. Others run deeper, like drinking, gambling, or infidelity. But no matter the size, all vices share one thing in common: they hold you back.

So, what's a bad habit? It's anything that takes more than it gives. If it doesn't support your growth or your well-being, it's worth asking whether it belongs in your life.

We all have habits that could be improved—or let go of altogether. That doesn't mean you need to go looking for flaws or overanalyze your every move. But when a chance to grow presents itself, it's worth paying attention.

Here are two powerful reasons to let go of a bad habit:

1. To make room for something better.

One reason to let go of a bad habit is simple: to make room for something better. We understand this when it comes to physical clutter—clearing out a junk drawer or letting go of clothes we never wear. The same idea applies to our habits.

If you're a smoker, for example, you know how much space it takes up—your time, your energy, even your health. The same goes for habits like overeating, doom-scrolling, or constantly checking your phone.

We give these habits a lot—but what do they really give us in return? Are they adding value?

Imagine what might open up if you took that back. You could feel clearer. More grounded. More connected to what matters.

What would you do with that kind of freedom?

2. Vices steal your control.

Vices rob us of our sovereignty—our ability to control our own life. When we fall into habits we don't consciously choose, we lose control of our time, energy, and decisions.

If you're giving time to distractions instead of your priorities, you're not choosing to invest in something meaningful—your time is simply slipping away. And that loss of personal sovereignty doesn't just affect your schedule. It creates stress, anxiety, and fatigue. It can creep into your relationships, your work, even your sense of self.

Bad habits—like junk food or screen addiction—drain your clarity, dull your motivation, and pull you further from the life you want. And if they're left unchecked, they snowball into bigger obstacles—harder to recognize, harder to break, and harder to climb out of.

The first step to breaking a bad habit is awareness. Recognizing your vices is half the battle. Once you can see them for what they really are—patterns that no longer serve you—you're already moving toward change.

Remember, it's about progress, not perfection. Change takes time. You won't break a habit overnight, but staying consistent is what matters. Even if it's just a few minutes a day, showing up builds momentum. Those small wins add up —and before long, the new habit will feel as automatic as the old one.

After you've identified a habit you want to change, don't feel like you have to go it alone. If you can handle it yourself, that's great. But if you need support, ask for it. Whether it's a friend, a therapist, or a support group, reaching out can make all the difference.

The key is being willing to do the work—to show up for the life you want. And sometimes, the hardest part is just getting started. We often avoid change because it feels uncomfortable. But that discomfort? It's a sign of growth. Whether you're cutting back on sugar or cutting down on screen time, the first step is always the hardest. But growth doesn't happen in your comfort zone.

Don't just remove a bad habit—replace it with something that builds the life you want. If you're cutting out TV time, try reading a book, learning a new skill, or getting outside for a walk. The key is consistency—each time you make a better choice, you strengthen your ability to change.

As you move forward, remember: we all have vices. It's part of being human—but it's also something we can change. When you spot a vice, name it. Then take steps to shift it. Fill that space with something better—something that fuels your growth.

Breaking a bad habit isn't punishment—it's an investment in yourself. Every step you take, no matter how small, brings you closer to a stronger, freer version of you. You have the power to shape your life—and it starts now. Let this be your advice to end a vice—because you're worth it.

Day 32.

Turn Knowledge Into Wisdom

"Knowledge won't change your life—but wisdom?
Wisdom will set you free."

Have you ever felt like you *should* know better—but didn't quite act like it?

That gap between knowing and doing is where wisdom lives.

Wisdom is important. It's the trademark of anyone who has achieved personal success on their journey. It's more than just accumulating knowledge—it's something deeper, something that shapes how we live, how we act, and how we respond to the world around us. Wisdom is what we gain when we master the art of living.

By now, chances are you've already accumulated a great deal of knowledge.

Knowledge is the information, facts, and data we've gathered throughout our lives. When you reflect on all that you know, it might feel like you're already well on your way to becoming a wise person. Right?

Maybe—but here's the thing: knowledge alone doesn't equal wisdom.

Knowledge is knowing. Wisdom is doing.

Knowledge is the foundation of wisdom; it's the raw material that wisdom is built from. We can possess vast amounts of knowledge, ace any trivia contest, or rattle off facts, but still lack wisdom. The key is to transform that knowledge into wisdom.

That's what makes wisdom the ultimate game-changer. It's knowledge in action—the difference between knowing how to drive a car and actually getting behind the wheel and driving. Even when we have what we need to reach a goal, knowledge alone isn't enough. Wisdom is what takes us to the next level; it's what moves us forward and turns our dreams into reality.

In order to make meaningful changes in our lives, we need more than facts and data—we need wisdom to take action on them. So, how do we become wise?

The answer is simple: we turn knowledge into wisdom.

It's a two-step process: **acquire knowledge** and **act on that knowledge.**

By reading this book and learning the methods and techniques inside, you're already doing step one—you're acquiring knowledge. But knowledge alone isn't enough. It's when you begin to apply what you know that you step into wisdom.

Take the example of learning to cook. At first, you might study the ingredients, the techniques, and the recipes. But knowing the theory behind cooking is different from actually preparing a meal. It's in the act of cooking—the chopping, the stirring, the adjusting of heat—that you truly turn that knowledge into wisdom. The recipe is just the starting point, but the experience of cooking is where the transformation happens. It's about taking what you know and using it to create something real and tangible. That's wisdom in action.

So, what now? A wise person might say, "I need to understand the changes I want to make—so I can become wise enough to make them." Wisdom doesn't keep track of what you know—it asks what you've done with it. It's not about having all the answers; it's about recognizing what you *don't* know and being willing to learn.

Becoming wise is an ongoing process that helps you navigate life's challenges, adapt to new situations, and become the best version of yourself.

And remember, true wisdom isn't just about knowing—it's about doing. So don't wait for the perfect moment. Take one piece of insight you've gained and act on it today. Start small. Test it. Let the experience shape you.

Because you don't gain wisdom by studying it—you gain it by living it.

True wisdom doesn't come from knowing more—it comes from doing more with what you've already learned. It's forged in practice, shaped by experience, and reflected in how you live your life.

Now, it's time to put your knowledge into action. Don't wait for everything to be perfect or for all the answers to be clear. One small action, applied to an area of your life, is all it takes to begin. This is how wisdom is born.

A wise person once said, "Turn knowledge into wisdom," and they were right.

The journey from knowledge to wisdom is yours—now go make it happen.

Day 33.

The Pain Game

"It may be part of your story, but it's not the whole story. Heal."

Many of us live with pain—whether it's physical, emotional, or spiritual. Some carry a little, while others endure a great deal. What truly matters, though, is what we choose to do with that pain. How we handle it determines how it shapes our lives—and whether it controls us or we control it.

Do we hang our pain in a closet, out of sight, hoping never to see it again? Or do we wear it like a sweater, letting it cling to us everywhere we go? Maybe we keep it locked away, only bringing it out for a therapist or a trusted friend. However we carry it, we have to ask—are we managing our pain, or is it managing us?

But here's the thing: life isn't about simply finding a way to coexist with pain or learning to work around it. We can deal with it, walk away from it, and move forward. Pain doesn't have to control us—and we don't have to center our lives around it. The "pain game" is what happens when we avoid, deny, or try to coexist with pain instead of making a plan to heal. It's when we let pain take up space in our lives without addressing it—hoping that it will somehow resolve itself. If you find yourself playing the pain game, it's time to make a change.

Living with pain can be like having a dysfunctional roommate. You share the same space, but things get messy when you both need to use the kitchen—someone's always in the way. You could avoid each other, staying in separate rooms, but no one thrives in isolation. Or worse, you could stay in your room while your pain takes over the house, leaving you lonely, resentful, and with your needs unmet.

So, how do we live with pain and still thrive? The answer: you can't. You need a plan for your pain. Trying to coexist with it—playing the "pain game"—is as futile as trying to thrive with a dysfunctional roommate. It doesn't work—and when you try, it only delays the inevitable. When pain is present, it must be dealt with.

Here's why: You can't bury pain—it will fester like mold in the dark, waiting for the right moment to surface. We see this when old wounds reemerge as bigger problems later in life. For example, marital issues stemming from watching your parents struggle; or unresolved childhood trauma that causes trust issues in relationships. Unhealed pain always finds a way to come back.

We can't live freely with pain either. Like roommates constantly bumping into each other, pain loves to make its presence known. PTSD is a perfect example—it's a constant reminder of what we're not allowed to do. Pain can't be left unchecked. Like addiction, pain demands attention before we can meet our own needs. Living with pain isn't sustainable. It needs to be addressed, and a plan must be made to deal with it.

The thing is, pain doesn't go away on its own. Like a room that's slowly filling with smoke, ignoring it only makes the situation worse. You can open a window and let in fresh air, but you first have to acknowledge the smoke is there. It's the same with pain—denying it or pretending it's not a problem doesn't make it disappear. The first step is facing it head-on. There's no shame in seeking help, whether from professionals or your own inner strength.

So, what's the solution? Well, it depends. Pain shows up differently for everyone—some kinds have spots, others have stripes, and some hitch a ride on your back. Don't make the mistake of thinking you can just live with it and that life will work around it—because it won't.

Understand this: without healing your pain, you're playing a pain game that always ends the same—with more pain. Recognize the pain, then decide how to deal with it. There are plenty of therapists, coaches, guides, and books to help you along your journey. Start by making a plan and ease into it.

Don't feel pressured to fix everything at once. Healing is about making small, deliberate steps forward. You don't need to have the entire map figured out. Start with what you know, and let that guide you. Sometimes, the biggest victories are found in the tiniest changes. Whether it's speaking up about your pain for the first time or simply acknowledging it, each step is an important part of your journey.

You don't have to play the pain game. While there's no magic trick to erasing pain, you do have the power to decide how you respond to it. You are not your pain—it may be written into your story, but it doesn't get to be the ending. You can choose to let it control you, or you can take charge of how it shapes you. The choice is yours.

You don't have to carry it forever. You don't have to let it win. Own your pain. Heal. You're in control now.

Day 34.

Pay Attention to Your Attention

"We're all stones in the weather—what we watch, read, and listen to will either wear us down or polish us. The choice is ours."

Pay attention.

Pay attention to *what*, exactly?

Pay attention to what's controlling your thoughts.

What's controlling your thoughts?

Whatever you choose to pay attention to.

Think about it.

Attention is power. Whoever—or whatever—you pay attention to has power over you. It shapes your focus, and in turn, it shapes your thoughts, your emotions, and your experiences—*everything*.

So, who or what are you giving your attention to? Are you glued to the TV, scrolling through social media, or lost in a book? How much time do you spend on these activities, and more importantly, what do you really know about the people you're engaging with? These questions matter because you cannot become who you truly desire to be unless you're the one controlling your thoughts and emotions. And that starts with carefully choosing where you focus your attention.

Have you ever had someone in your life who wasn't a good influence—someone you had to spend less time around because you didn't like the person you became when they were around? Most of us have had this kind of person in our lives— and some of us still do. It's crucial to be mindful of how we spend our time, because we tend to mirror what we focus on. If we spend time watching the news, we start to take on the perspectives of the newscasters. If we're drawn to certain social media posts, we might share them—and start adopting the views those posts represent. If YouTube videos captivate us, they start to shape our conversations—and even our opinions.

This is why children are not allowed to watch inappropriate content—they tend to believe what they see and often imitate what they watch. The same is true for adults, though our imitations are often subconscious. Have you ever noticed how you treat others more kindly after being around people who are kind to you? Or how your energy shifts after watching an action-packed movie or a sporting event? What about after listening to an enthusiastic speaker? If we aren't careful, we become what we focus on.

As adults, we don't always have someone telling us what we should or shouldn't consume. That responsibility is ours. It's easy to forget that what we expose ourselves to—whether it's the headlines, the conversations we engage in, or the content we watch—still shapes us. The good news is, we have the power to shift our focus toward the influences that motivate us, support our growth, and align with our values and goals.

That's why it's so important to consciously choose where we direct our attention. If we don't, we risk shaping ourselves after people or influences we don't want to imitate. Ask yourself:

- How do I spend my free time?

- Who do I spend most of my time around?

- Where do I turn for advice?

- Who do I trust?

You, me, the neighborhood—we're all like stones in the weather. The shows we watch, the material we read, and the people we listen to are like raindrops falling on us. They'll either wear us down or polish us, shaping who we become.

The choice is ours. The people and things we allow into our circle of influence are completely within our control, which means it's our responsibility to choose wisely.

It's not about whether you watch TV or scroll social media—it's about understanding the power of your attention and using it to your advantage. Know that your thoughts, personality, and beliefs will eventually reflect where your focus goes. So choose wisely. Direct your attention toward who you want to become. Observe what you're observing—and if you make the right choices, you'll begin to see a reflection of your ideal self in the world around you.

Day 35.

Move the Bar

"The people who thrive in life hold themselves to higher standards and boldly ask for what they truly deserve—without hesitation."

Do you have standards—guiding principles or rules that help you determine what's acceptable in your life?

If you do, how do you decide where to set the bar? Is there a method you use to determine what's right for you?

How do you choose the right job? Do you first establish a salary range that meets your needs, then select a job within that range? How do you decide where to live or what qualities you look for in a partner?

We've all made choices without clear standards to guide us—only to find ourselves in relationships that drained us or jobs that didn't fulfill us. For me, it wasn't until I turned forty that I realized some of the situations I wasn't proud of were directly linked to the standards I had set for myself. Too often, I had set the bar too low, settling for less than I deserved—or, worse, setting standards so low that they allowed abuse, neglect, and a compromise of my happiness.

Once I realized that my standards determined what I accepted into my life, I understood that I was the one in control of where I set the bar. And with that control comes the power to avoid undesirable situations, such as:

- Jobs that don't support your financial stability

- Friends or family who treat you poorly

- Unfulfilling relationships that drain more than they give

- Living spaces that feel more stressful than safe

- Constant stress from managing crises instead of creating joy

- Accepting poor physical or mental health as your normal

- Always running late and feeling behind

- Low self-esteem that keeps you small

If any of this sounds familiar, it's time to move the bar. It's time to reevaluate what's truly acceptable in your life and adjust accordingly. If we aren't actively choosing our own standards, outside influences may be setting them for us.

When we accept situations below our potential, we're not just settling for less—we're also telling ourselves that we're not worthy of more. Moving the bar is about shifting that narrative. It's about stepping into your true potential and recognizing that you deserve nothing less than a happy life. The people who thrive in life are those who hold themselves to higher standards, and they've learned how to ask for what they deserve without hesitation. You deserve that too.

When we don't take charge of our standards, we often fall back on what we were taught growing up or what we've experienced. Our parents, schools, and social institutions shape what we believe we deserve, influencing our values and expectations. Similarly, our past experiences—whether with employers, coworkers, or in relationships—set the bar for how we think we should be treated. This may work out fine if we had the best role models. But what if we didn't? What if some of the values we adopted no longer align with what's best for us today? When we don't consciously set our own standards, we let others do it for us, often leaving our happiness to chance.

What I've learned after forty years of mixed outcomes is simple: I must ask for exactly what I need and want. This is how I set the bar. It's the only way I can be sure I'm living the life I want for myself.

Start saying things like, "I will choose a job that allows me to thrive," or "I will choose a partner who challenges me and treats me with the respect I deserve." Don't be afraid to set your standards high and ask for what you want. You're worth it—never forget that!

As you reflect on the standards you currently live by, don't feel discouraged. Don't tell yourself, "I messed up by setting the bar too low." Everything happens for a reason, and if you're not happy with the choices you've made in the past, use those lessons to help you move forward. If you look closely, you'll see how your journey has prepared you to raise the bar even higher. Don't dwell on missed chances. Use them as fuel for your next decision. Because all the mistakes and successes of your life have been laid before you like stepping stones, bringing you to this very moment. This is your time.

The best thing you can do today is move the bar. Raise your standards, accept nothing less than happiness, and live with the intention to soar. The life you deserve is within reach.

Day 36.

Just Be

"If we can't be alone with ourselves, here's the question to ask: What are we really afraid to face?"

Picture this: after a long day at work, you walk through the front door, flick on the lights, and collapse into your favorite chair. Now ask yourself—how long until the television comes on? How long before you check your phone, tablet, or another device? Can you sit still for five minutes? Is thirty minutes of doing nothing even possible? An hour? Can you tolerate the silence of your own company—and if so, do you have the patience to just *be*?

I remember a conversation I had with a friend. We were catching up, talking about nothing in particular, when he mentioned he'd been frustrated lately because he couldn't find anything to watch on TV. To give some context: we both loved movies and television shows and were always on the lookout for something new to watch. The only difference was, at that point, I no longer watched TV—and I hadn't shared this with him yet.

"I can't help you," I told him. "I haven't kept up with shows lately," which, at the time, was an understatement. It had been over a year and a half since I'd watched anything at all. The truth is, I had come to love "me time," and silence was something I'd grown to deeply enjoy.

"I live alone," he replied. "I can't just sit in silence—it'll drive me crazy."

My friend couldn't just be. The idea of solitude without something to entertain him was unthinkable. But why is that? Why do we shy away from idle time? I used to be the same way—I'd turn on music or the TV as soon as I walked through the door, just to fill the quiet and avoid facing my own thoughts. But now, silence is something I look forward to. I remember a time when I had a medical emergency that kept me in the hospital for several days. Despite being alone, the screen stayed off—the distraction it once offered no longer felt necessary. And surprisingly, I didn't miss it. There were ample reminders of where I was—the beeping of machines, the scurrying of hospital staff—but I found comfort in the silence of that room. When they told me I was going home, I felt grateful but also thought, "I'm going to miss the quiet." And I really did.

In our fast-paced world, silence can seem like a luxury or even a challenge. We're constantly surrounded by noise— whether it's from the media, conversations, or the constant hum of technology. But the truth is, silence offers something we often overlook: clarity. In the stillness, we have the space to hear ourselves think without distraction. And in that space, we can reflect, process emotions, and find solutions that we didn't realize we were searching for. Silence isn't just a break from noise—it's a chance to hear ourselves more clearly.

Many of us avoid silence because it forces us to be alone with our thoughts—which means it's not the silence we're truly avoiding, but ourselves. When we can't sit still, there's often something in our lives that we haven't made peace with—something we're reluctant to confront. Our thoughts remind us of our reality, so when we avoid the quiet, we're really avoiding our reality. If we can't be alone with ourselves, here's the question to ask: *What are we avoiding?*

One of the gifts of silence is that it holds space for us to uncover the things we need to work through. Sometimes, it can be uncomfortable to sit with our emotions or thoughts, but it's in these moments that we gain insight into the areas of our lives that need attention. When we resist the urge to turn on the TV or scroll through our phones, we're giving ourselves permission to pause and reflect. It's in these pauses that we can begin to heal and shift our perspectives. The more we practice this, the easier it becomes to embrace the quiet and allow our minds to wander, without fear of what we might discover.

If you find it difficult to be alone with your thoughts, it might be helpful to explore why. Spend time in stillness and see what comes up. Use it as an opportunity to check in with yourself and take note of where you are. If you feel at peace, you'll likely notice a sense of calm, free from irritation or anxiety. But if certain thoughts make you uneasy or uncomfortable, pay attention to them. These are the areas asking for your attention and care.

Remember, when you are at peace with yourself, you'll love being in your own company. You'll enjoy the practice of just being. Why not give it a try? Spend time simply being with yourself—use this time as a check-in. Whatever surfaces will be worth exploring. And if nothing troubling arises? You might just discover one of your new favorite things to do. Guaranteed.

Give it a try—and may you find the peace that's been waiting for you all along.

Day 37.

Be Brave

"Bravery is the key to a healthy mindset—it's our shield against the toxic grip of worry, fear, and stress."

Would you consider yourself brave? Do you meet challenges head-on, or do you hesitate when things feel uncertain? I'm not just talking about the fun stuff—like trying a new recipe or planning a spontaneous trip—but also the tough stuff: the moments that stretch you, like stepping into the spotlight, showing up when it's uncomfortable, or facing something you've been putting off. Bravery isn't just for emergencies or big decisions—it's a mindset, and it can shape the way you handle everything from everyday stress to life's bigger turning points.

So, why should we be courageous? What makes facing the unknown with anticipation, rather than anxiety, worth it?

We seek bravery because it's key to maintaining a healthy mindset. It shields us from the toxic effects of worry, fear, and stress. Life is always in motion—nothing stays the same, and everything flows from one moment to the next.

Every breath is a fresh start. Every heartbeat, a new beginning. Think of life as a circle that's constantly resetting. Now, imagine that circle on a smaller scale: every day begins a new cycle. It starts when you wake up, moves through the morning, flows into lunch, and continues until the day ends with sleep. Ask yourself: how many experiences unfold in a day? How many fresh starts?

The truth is, every moment offers a new start, and each thought is an opportunity. We want to face these moments without fear, without the weight of anxiety or dread. When we approach experiences with fear or stress, we let them overshadow what could be peaceful, enjoyable moments. If we allow fear to take the lead, we may unknowingly live in a constant state of apprehension. Bravery isn't something we should practice only occasionally; it's a necessity for our mental and physical health. We are always stepping into the unknown—whether we realize it or not. And when fear holds us back, even in the smallest moments, it influences every decision, big or small. These little doses of fear accumulate over time.

I used to feel overwhelming fear and anxiety in situations others might find simple, like running into someone I knew in public. Even with familiar faces, I'd freeze up, worrying about how I looked, if they'd judge me, or if I'd say the wrong thing. The fear wasn't just about the interaction —it was the uncertainty of how it would go. Often, I'd avoid people altogether, which only made my anxiety worse. Over time, I realized this fear was exhausting and holding me back. When I started facing those moments with courage instead of avoidance, the weight of my fear lightened, and I saw how much I had been limiting myself.

Imagine that each experience is like a drop of rain filling a bucket. Every time you take action, you either add a drop of fear or a drop of courage. You carry that bucket with you throughout the day, and by nightfall, it's full. At the end of the day, will you be weighed down by fear, or will your load feel lighter because courage isn't heavy? Most of us prefer a lighter load, and those lighter loads come when we choose anticipation and goodwill over fear.

Remember, habits are often unconscious, so it's important to form the right ones. When we live with the habit of making decisions from a place of fear or uncertainty, we often don't realize we're doing it until it's already affected our mental and physical health—contributing to elevated stress, worry, and doubt. But by choosing to live from a place of courage and excitement, we can transform our lives— improving our health, our mindset, and our everyday experiences.

Courage is like a daily vitamin—something we need to take consistently to strengthen our resilience. Just like vitamins strengthen our body, courage strengthens our mind —building a lasting foundation of peace and happiness. When we recognize fear's toll on our lives, we also see how the simple act of choosing bravery—day after day—creates a powerful shift. Instead of being reactive to stress and worry, we start proactively living with a mindset that embraces new experiences with openness and anticipation.

When we realize we're always in a state of starting fresh, we can approach life with open arms, a grateful heart, and an attitude of acceptance. By choosing courage every day, we can replace the negative byproducts of fear—stress, worry, low confidence—with the healthy side effects of happiness: joy, excitement, and peace.

A home is only as strong as its foundation. When we build from a foundation of fear, the structure we create lacks the integrity we need. But when we build from happiness— from a foundation of bravery—we create something that will support us for a lifetime. And everything we build upon it will stand the test of time.

Day 38.

Flow

---

*"When you stop resisting the natural rhythm of life,
everything gets easier—even the hard stuff."*

Do you know what it really means to "flow"—as in, to
be in a "flow state" or to "go with the flow"? It's a buzzword
we hear a lot these days, often tied to doing what feels
natural and effortless in day-to-day life. But what does it
really mean to flow?

Flowing means letting yourself be carried by the
path you're on, without resistance. It's about moving
through your day with ease, gliding from one moment to
the next. Living in a flow state is one of the most blissful
ways to experience life, and it's something we all long to
feel. But to truly live in this state, we first need to
understand what it really involves.

Think about flowing water—a stream moving
naturally with gravity. If something blocks its path, like a
boulder, it doesn't fight it. Instead, the water flows over or
around the obstacle, gradually eroding it until there's no

resistance left. While storms and heavy rains can disrupt its course, the water always finds its way, and the flow eventually smooths out.

Life is meant to move like this—effortless, rhythmic, and free. But this doesn't mean passively accepting whatever comes our way. Instead, it's about continuing to move forward, despite obstacles, without unnecessary stress. Like water flowing over rocks, we face challenges with ease, knowing they don't define us. We don't let life push us off course—unless we choose to change direction ourselves. We simply flow, trusting that we are moving in the right direction.

When you're in a flow state, time seems to behave differently. It stretches and shrinks all at once. One moment, hours have passed without you even noticing; the next, a single moment feels like it lasts an eternity. It's as if time loses its grip on you, becoming something that flows with you rather than controlling your pace. This is the magic of flow: it creates a sense of timelessness, where you have nowhere to be yet feel exactly where you should be.

When you're fully immersed in what you're doing—whether it's writing, cooking, woodworking, or even having a meaningful conversation—you become so absorbed in the present that the ticking of the clock fades into the background. In these moments, you're not waiting for time to pass; you're simply living in the now—unhurried, content. Losing track of time is a key sign you're in a true flow state—a moment where you're no longer bound by the past or future but are fully immersed in the present.

Try this: Choose something you love that helps you lose yourself in the moment—and just do it. It can be anything you're passionate about—singing, running, fixing a car—just pick something you enjoy. Once you experience it, use that feeling as a baseline to gauge your other experiences. It gives you a sense of what you're aiming for—and a reminder that it's possible.

When you're in flow, it isn't just about feeling good in the moment—there are real benefits. You become fully present, free from distractions and tension, and as a result, you're more productive and creative. Flow also boosts your mood by releasing dopamine, which helps keep you motivated. The more you experience flow, the clearer your thinking becomes, stress fades, and you feel more connected to what truly matters. Life just feels easier and more rewarding.

Being in a flow state means allowing life to carry you where it will. You don't get upset, anxious, or afraid. Instead, you observe, allow, and move through life as effortlessly as water.

When you're in a flow state, the quality of your work improves naturally. You become fully absorbed in what you're doing, with no distractions or overthinking. You're able to focus deeply on the task at hand, and creativity emerges naturally. There's no stress or second-guessing, just a sense of trust in your abilities. As a result, your work feels more authentic, refined, and aligned with your true potential, almost like it's unfolding exactly as it should.

Are you in a flow state? If not, you can be—and it's worth striving for. Once you learn to go with the natural rhythm of life, everything becomes easier to navigate. You create a path that reflects who you are and leads toward what you truly want—and as you do, the world begins to open up.

Challenges will still arise, but instead of feeling overwhelmed, you'll meet them with a sense of calm and confidence. The more you embrace this flow, the more effortless life becomes.

You stop worrying about the how or the when—you simply trust that things will unfold at the right time. And that feeling, that freedom, is incredibly rewarding. Doesn't that sound like the life you've always wanted? You can have it today—just flow.

Day 39.

Have Patience

"When your life mirrors your desires, your desires start to mirror your life."

Have patience.

With what?

With everything. Especially yourself. Here's the surprising truth: slowing down can actually get you where you want to go faster.

Let me explain. I had a conversation recently that really stuck with me. A woman was talking about her friend, who had gone through a tough divorce and was struggling to start fresh. She told her friend not to give up on love, even though things hadn't worked out the first time. "There's happiness out there for you," she said.

I thought, "That's a nice, encouraging thing to say." But then, I was taken aback by what she said next.

"Just don't look now," she told her friend.

I was puzzled. "Why would she say that?" I wondered. "Isn't love out there for everyone? Shouldn't we always be on the lookout for love?"

Then she explained. "I kindly told her to work on her problems first," she said. "If she found someone new right now, she might end up with someone like the person she just left."

At first, I thought, "Was that really the advice she needed to hear?" But as I reflected on it, I realized there might be something to this bold suggestion. Here's the thing: Let's say she wants a nonsmoker, but she's currently a smoker. She might attract one, but her chances would increase if she quit smoking. If she wants someone who exercises, wouldn't it make sense for her to start working out herself? The more she aligns with the kind of partner she's looking for, the better her chances of attracting that person.

That's when I laughed to myself and thought, "This person might be a genius." Like attracts like. The more you embody the qualities or lifestyle you want in a partner—or in anything else—the more likely you are to draw it in.

It's not just about relationships, either. The same principle applies to careers or anything you want to welcome into your life. For example, if you want a particular job, don't just wait for the job to come to you. Start acquiring the skills that will make you the perfect candidate. If your dream is to travel the world, it's more likely to come true if you start saving money, researching destinations, and taking small trips. It's about merging your life with the reality you want. When your life mirrors your desires, your desires start to mirror your life.

That's when I had my aha moment: Patience. We don't have to rush to get what we want. We can attract the life we dream of—it just takes time and intention. The method is simple: become the person who aligns with the life you want. And then I was reminded of a wise adage: *Become the end result that you seek.* It's a phrase many people say, but here's what it really means: The universe will surround you with people, places, and opportunities that match your world. So, make your world reflect everything you desire. It might take time, but think about it—what's the rush? Isn't the life you want worth the wait? Of course it is!

But here's what many people miss: patience doesn't mean being passive. It's not about sitting back and waiting for life to hand you what you want. Patience is the balance between taking action and trusting that the timing will align. The key is staying engaged in the process without clinging to the outcome. You might start a new project, develop your skills, or take steps toward your goals, but if you're constantly anxious about how quickly things will unfold, you'll miss the point. Your efforts should flow naturally, free from the pressure of an urgent deadline. You can't force the sky to rain, but you can make sure you have an umbrella ready. Take someone who wants to buy a home, for example. They can't just wait for the perfect house to appear—they need to become the type of person who is ready for that commitment. This could mean improving their credit score, saving for a down payment, or learning about the home-buying process. It's not about rushing the market or forcing a deal. It's about aligning with the reality they want—and becoming a prepared, responsible buyer. By staying patient, working on themselves, and trusting that the right opportunity will come when they're ready, they'll be in the best position to seize it when the time is right.

Start by thinking about who you want to be and what you want your life to look like. Then, start moving in that direction with a clear plan. Take small steps, gradually molding yourself into the person who reflects the life you desire. And trust your intuition—it knows what's best for you.

Lastly, when I think back on that conversation about love and relationships, I realize something important: always be aware of your surroundings, because you never know when you'll encounter a moment of divine wisdom. You might hear something you barely notice at first... and then it echoes through your life forever.

Day 40.

Decisions, Decisions, Decisions

"At every moment, we're either moving toward self-love or away from it. It's that simple."

Do you ever feel overwhelmed by all the decisions you have to make? Most of us do! With so many choices packed into every day—what to eat, what to do, what to think, what to say, how to feel, how to act... and even when to breathe—it's easy to feel exhausted. Multiply that by everything we go through in a single day: waking up, getting ready, eating, commuting, working—and suddenly, we're making thousands —possibly even tens of thousands—of decisions before the day is done.

If we view each decision as a chance to either mess up or get it right, it's no wonder we feel drained. Of course we're tired!

With so many choices, it can seem like life is just a lottery ticket, but it doesn't have to feel that way. Instead of worrying about whether we're "getting it right," we can view each decision as an opportunity to move in the right direction.

After all, if we keep redirecting ourselves toward the right path, won't we eventually end up where we want to be?

When you get down to it, we really only ever make two decisions: love or fear. It may sound strange, but think about it. Every choice we face is like standing at a crossroads: 1) choose love—take the path that nourishes your soul, brings you joy, and moves you closer to what you desire most, or 2) choose fear—take the route that avoids what's best, leading to difficulty and pushing you further from your true desires.

At every moment, we're either moving toward self-love or away from it. It's that simple.

It's like walking through life with an internal compass. You can choose to follow the magnetic pull toward self-love, or you can let fear take you in the opposite direction. A good way to tell the difference is this: when you're moving away from self-love, it doesn't feel good. You might feel a brief sense of comfort, but underneath it all, you'll feel disconnected or uneasy. On the other hand, when you choose love—even in small ways—it adds up, and you start feeling more in tune with yourself.

Take breakfast, for example. What do you eat when you wake up in the morning? These days, I usually go for oatmeal —not the instant kind, but the stovetop variety, boiled to mushy perfection. It's not exciting, but it's incredibly healthy. It takes effort: I have to deal with dirty dishes, make it from scratch, measure the water and oats, add ingredients for flavor, and wait for it to cook. It's definitely not as fast as cereal or other quick options. The point is: oatmeal requires effort.

In my earlier years, I would have chosen cereal, a breakfast bar, or, on my laziest days, a protein shake. But now, I choose love for my body and mind over the fear of a little work. And honestly, it feels really satisfying.

The truth is, even if you find yourself heading in a direction you don't want to go, it's not necessarily bad. Sometimes, we need to experience what we don't want to truly understand what we do want. We have to be kind to ourselves. As long as we remain aware of the choices we're making, there are no wrong turns—just detours along the way.

Do you see how it works? Every moment presents an opportunity to move closer to your desires or further away from them. When you shift your perspective, you'll be amazed at how quickly your life starts to change. Break your choices down to their simplest forms—love or fear. Reflect on where your decisions fall, and imagine what they might look like if you chose the other path. If you're not happy with the results, you'll know how to choose differently next time.

Think about the relationships in your life. We often make decisions about how to respond to others based on fear —fear of conflict, fear of judgment, or fear of not being understood. But imagine how much more open and authentic your relationships could be if you chose love instead. Love might look like having the tough conversation with someone instead of avoiding it. Or, love might be setting boundaries with people who drain your energy. When you choose love in your relationships, you're not only nurturing those connections, but you're also nurturing your own sense of self-respect and worth.

I promise you, once you realize that love and fear are the only two roads you ever travel, everything starts to make sense. You'll no longer see life as a series of "decisions, decisions, decisions." Instead, everything becomes "opportunities, opportunities, opportunities." And the world begins to fall into place.

Day 41.

Not Your Problem

"Carrying other people's problems weighs more than you think. It's time to put them down."

Do you remember your childhood friends—the ones who felt like family? Did you ever go to bat for them? Keep their secrets, take their side, or get into trouble on their behalf? I know I did.

And as you got older, did you ever feel deeply affected by things that had nothing to do with you directly? Maybe you felt drawn to causes, stood up for others, or got caught up in things that weren't really yours to fix.

It's fine to "take one for the team" when you're young—it's part of growing up and learning. But as adults, this tendency should be left behind. Everything we do carries emotional weight, and when we get caught up in other people's problems, we end up carrying baggage that's not ours to bear. This can lead to stress, weight gain, sleepless nights, anxiety, and distractions—the list goes on. But the truth is, all of these things are avoidable.

That's not to say we shouldn't help others or practice goodwill—because we definitely should. But we need to be selective about what we take on. If a situation isn't something you can directly improve, is it worth getting involved? Sometimes, sure. But more often than not, the answer is no.

It's easy to get caught up in other people's dramas, especially when they touch on emotions we're sensitive to— like anger, sadness, frustration, or fear. But think about it: when you invest your energy in problems that aren't yours, how often do you feel empowered afterward? Most of the time, it's the opposite—you feel drained, unsettled, or even confused. It's like carrying someone else's luggage for miles— you're tired, and it's not even your bag to carry. Practicing the art of saying "no" isn't just about avoiding stress—it's about protecting your emotional space from burdens that aren't yours to take on.

Here are a few common situations where adopting a "not my problem" mindset can be helpful:

- Workplace gossip
- Disagreements that don't involve you
- Speculation without evidence
- Private conversations that aren't for you
- Hurtful opinions
- Prying for personal information

- Matters that don't affect you or the people discussing them

When we find ourselves in these situations, we're allowed to step back and let those moments pass without getting pulled in. We don't have to make these issues part of our reality. If you're unsure how to step back, here are a few responses that can help:

- "I don't know about that."
- "That's none of my business."
- "I'm not comfortable talking about that."
- "I don't have an opinion on that."
- "I'd rather not say."
- "I don't like to get involved in personal matters."

Remember, things like gossip, speculation, or unwelcome opinions are just extra baggage someone else is trying to hand you. You don't have to pick it up. By adopting a "not my problem" mindset, you protect your energy and stay focused on what's truly yours.

Life is already demanding enough with our own problems. We don't need to carry someone else's. Walking away from those situations isn't just okay—it's recommended. When you practice this mindset, you'll see how the challenges in your life become more manageable, focused only on what's truly yours.

Over time, as you handle your own problems without absorbing those of others, you'll feel lighter, freer, and more able to focus on the life you want to build.

So, try it—have fewer problems in your life. If you haven't already, you'll quickly notice the freedom that comes with it. The clarity, the peace of mind, and the energy you regain will be undeniable. You'll wonder why you didn't make the shift sooner.

Day 42.

From Knots to Knowing

"The path to knowing yourself often begins with untangling what you're not."

Maybe you've felt it—that quiet sense that something's off. Not always a crisis, just a tension. A heaviness you can't quite name.

Life has a way of tying itself into knots. Some are obvious—burnout, emotional exhaustion, the moment you realize something just isn't working. But others are quieter. Habits that once protected you but now hold you back. Roles you've outgrown. Doubts you've carried for years without realizing it.

These knots can shape how you show up, what you settle for, and what you believe you deserve. And often, we don't even notice them—until we do.

That's where the real work begins. Untangling isn't easy. But it's where clarity lives—not just about life, but about *you*. Because at the heart of every knot you loosen is a deeper understanding of who you are becoming.

As you continue to untangle these parts of your life, remember to meet yourself with honesty and compassion. This isn't just about letting go—it's about knowing yourself more deeply. That's the real gift beneath every challenge.

Just like brushing through knotted hair—what matters is that you take your time. You don't need the scissors. You don't need to start over. You just begin where you are—gently, patiently—working through what's been stuck. This process requires compassion, not force. It's about choosing kindness, even when you're frustrated. Recognize what feels tight or misaligned. Then begin, step by step, until things start to fall into place. There's no rush. Life isn't a race. Move at your own pace, and you'll get where you're meant to be when the time is right.

The things that hold us back can look different for everyone. Take weight gain, for instance—the freshman twenty, the holiday fifteen, the depression thirty (maybe even the depression fifty!). Most of us have been there.

Lasting progress happens at a healthy pace. Rushing can leave us depleted or burned out—physically, emotionally, even spiritually. In situations like this, it's best to take it one step at a time—paying attention to what's driving your habits, what your body's asking for, and what kind of care you've actually been needing all along.

But it's not just personal habits that get tangled. Sometimes the friction shows up at work—low pay, toxic environments, or zero room for growth. It wears on you. But leaving without a plan can make things worse. Before acting, slow down. Untangle the frustration. Get clear on what matters—what you value, what you're done tolerating, and what kind of life you want to build next.

Some knots go deeper than routine or environment. Some are woven into how we see ourselves—especially when our worth depends on someone else. It's painful, and often hard to recognize until you feel completely drained or lost. So how do you begin to shift that? Gently. Start with self-love— not in theory, but in practice. Get honest about how you truly feel about yourself when no one else is around. That's where the real work begins.

From here, you can begin laying the groundwork for something stronger—something rooted in truth and self-respect. Spend quality time with yourself. Take up hobbies. Have "me time" and engage in activities that nurture a deeper connection with who you truly are. Reflect on how comfortable you are standing on your own, and identify areas where you can become more self-sufficient and confident in your ability to provide for yourself. If your happiness depends on others' well-being, it becomes conditional. Strengthen your ability to navigate life independently, taking it slow—one step at a time.

There was a time when my happiness was completely entangled with someone else's approval. I believed love would fill something hollow in me. I kept giving, but it was never enough. The love I received felt transactional—like something bought and paid for—and the demands kept growing. The more I tried to please, the more lost I became. Eventually, I saw the pattern of external validation for what it was. I wasn't just giving too much—I was holding onto something that wasn't even real.

It took time and patience, but I began to untangle the parts of myself I had lost in the process. I reconnected with the simple joys I had forgotten—making music, being outdoors, embracing my role as a father. Slowly, I loosened the patterns of codependency, set boundaries, and realized my worth didn't depend on anyone else. Letting go of that deeply rooted need for validation was one of the hardest yet most freeing things I've ever done.

I didn't fix it all at once. But I stayed with it. And that's what made the difference. So when something in your life feels tight, heavy, or off, don't rush to cut it out. Take the time to see it clearly. Work through it with care. Every step is a chance to understand yourself more deeply.

Be patient. Be compassionate. Stay your own biggest cheerleader.

That's the journey from knots to knowing—untangling what no longer serves you, and seeing, maybe for the first time, who you truly are beneath it all.

Day 43.

A Well-Oiled Machine

"Every day, every choice, every lesson—they all play a part in the unfolding of you."

By now, you've come a long way. Take a moment to reflect: Can you feel the shift? Are these chapters helping you grow into the person you've been working so hard to become?

At this point, you've absorbed a lot—new ideas, fresh perspectives, and tools that can truly change your life. Hopefully, you've built a solid foundation for the future you envision. Embrace the practices that resonate, and make them your own. As you begin thinking and acting like the person you're stepping into, you'll naturally start attracting the experiences that mirror that version of you. Over time, you'll find yourself moving with more clarity and ease—momentum will carry you forward.

When your efforts start aligning—your thoughts, habits, and intentions working in sync—something powerful happens. Things begin to flow. Progress feels steady. Like a well-oiled machine, your growth gains traction. The small steps you've taken start to add up, and the pieces fall into place.

That's what it feels like when your inner and outer worlds start moving in harmony. Your values, actions, relationships, work, and purpose begin pointing in the same direction— toward something meaningful. You're no longer forcing progress—it's unfolding, because you're in sync with who you truly are. And when that happens—and trust me, it will—life begins to feel less like a struggle and more like a rhythm.

Of course, that doesn't mean everything will be easy. Growth is ongoing, and challenges will still arise. But with the tools you've gained, you'll be more than equipped to meet those moments with resilience and grace.

Some days will feel more impactful than others—and that's okay. Like the ingredients in a great recipe, every moment has its purpose. Some are bold, some subtle, but all of them matter. Each experience becomes part of the whole— helping shape the person you're becoming. It's not about getting everything right—it's about allowing it all to come together in a way that makes sense for you. Bit by bit, the new you begins to emerge.

Growth isn't just about collecting ideas—it's about engaging with them. Journaling your progress and reflecting on what resonates can be incredibly helpful. Write down your insights, underline passages that stand out, and make notes in the margins. Some might shy away from marking up a book, but I see it as a sign of commitment. It shows you're not just reading—you're participating in your own evolution.

Remember: the version of you that's emerging is shaped by all the pieces you've gathered along the way. Let them come together. Let them build something beautiful. That's what moves you forward.

It's easy to feel impatient with your progress or wonder if it's happening fast enough. But transformation doesn't happen all at once. Like a painting, it unfolds in layers. Every brushstroke matters. Each step you take—even the quiet, uncertain ones—contributes to the bigger picture. Trust the process. Be patient with yourself. What you're building is real, and it's taking shape beautifully.

Above all, remember this: continued personal growth is what brings depth and meaning to your life. The insights you've gathered will keep you centered and aligned with your deeper purpose, giving you strength when challenges come. Keep flowing. Stay open. And like a well-oiled machine— where everything works together with ease and intention—let your growth carry you forward, one meaningful step at a time.

One day, you'll look back and barely recognize who you used to be—not because you were lacking, but because of how far you've come.

Day 44.

It's All for You

"You were never here to live someone else's dream."

Do you know how special you are? You are the center of your own universe—your life's experiences revolve around you. Anything less will always feel incomplete. The truth is: it's all for you. This is your personal golden rule—the law of your world—and the very thing that will carry you through when everything else is unclear. Never forget it: it's all for you.

As you move through your days, months, and years, keep this truth in mind: *it's all for you.* Your joys, your struggles, everything you've ever worked for—the culmination of all your life experiences—have all been for you. Despite the joy on your parents' faces when you were born, you were not theirs. You entered this world as their child, but you are, and always have been, your own person. Your life is yours to live—not for your spouse, your friends, or your job. You are here for yourself. Just don't lose sight of that.

But let's clarify something important—maybe you're thinking, "That's not true—everything I do is for my children, my spouse, or my job." But let's pause for a moment and reflect: if caring for others didn't offer you a sense of meaning or purpose, would you still do it in the same way?

Sometimes we give so much of ourselves—not just out of love, but also because the idea of *not* showing up causes us discomfort. Sit with that for a moment—this may be a new way of looking at things. Ask yourself: *What's really driving the choices I make?* You may realize that, in one way or another, it's all ultimately for you.

Let's explore a few real-life examples. Have you ever bought a home or lived in a certain area for someone else—someone who wanted to be there more than you, so you gave in? If so, how long did it take before you started longing for somewhere new? Was your love for that person enough to keep you in a place you didn't truly want to be? Think back to when you were younger—were you truly free to choose your own path despite your parents' influence? If you were, did you feel resistance before you could be yourself fully? Were you ever truly free to be yourself?

If the life you build—the paths you choose—isn't entirely for you, you will never feel complete. There will always be a sense of restlessness, a wondering about what could have been. This is crucial, because if you don't choose to live for yourself, something inside will keep pulling you back until you do. When you remember this, your choices are more likely to bring you peace and fulfillment. To live with clarity, without regret, you must fully realize that it's all for you.

Now, you might be thinking, "Isn't it selfish to put yourself first? Shouldn't I set aside my own desires for the sake of others?" The truth is, while putting your happiness last might seem noble, it often leads to resentment and burnout. But when you prioritize your well-being and follow what genuinely fulfills you, you become more whole—and from that place, you have so much more to give. It's not selfishness; it's self-care. And without that, you can't truly be there for others in a meaningful, sustainable way.

Take me, for example. A few years ago, I was working long hours and juggling multiple jobs that, while providing a good living, left me exhausted. I kept telling myself that the hours I was putting in were for my family—that it was my responsibility to provide. But the truth was, I was choosing work over myself. I had pushed aside the passions that once made me feel alive. I was trading my life for what I thought I was supposed to do, and eventually, my body let me know. A health crisis forced me to stop—and in that space, I realized something had to change. I began dedicating time to the things that mattered to me: writing, creating, and spending more time with my kids. It wasn't easy, and at first, I felt guilty for not constantly working. But once I made the shift, I found that I was not only happier—I was also more present and able to give fully to the people I love. Most importantly, I became a better dad. It was a lesson in realizing that when you prioritize your own happiness, you become better for everyone around you, too.

Putting yourself first isn't always easy. When you do, it can feel like you're neglecting other priorities. But that doesn't mean you've abandoned those you love, nor does it mean their lives are diminished. What it truly means is that if you don't put your own needs first—if you don't pursue the passions that make your soul come alive—you will either end up doing so eventually, or you may come to resent the people for whom you sacrificed your own joy. Remember, it's natural to seek out what brings you fulfillment. Anything less leads to suffering. We are not meant to suffer, but to thrive. It's the natural course of life to move toward what nourishes the soul.

Now, you've arrived at the graduate-level question of putting yourself first: "How do we care for others while still honoring ourselves?" The answer is simple: we find a way to pursue what matters to us while continuing to care for those we love. And if we can't do both, then caring for others must become something we *genuinely* want—not something we do out of guilt or obligation. This is the key to happiness. When you find meaning in what you do—because you're doing it for yourself—you experience a deeper, more lasting contentment. And if you're not finding joy or satisfaction in what you're doing, it's worth asking: *Am I doing this for the right reasons?*

Why waste time, energy, effort, money, or love on anything that isn't truly for you? Putting yourself first now can save you from years of wandering down paths that aren't aligned with who you really are. When you choose to put yourself first, you give yourself permission to experience the happiness, joy, and fulfillment you deserve. Life is too short to live for anyone but yourself. So, when you plan your future, make sure it's infused with the things that bring you to life. When you do, you'll find yourself filled with such deep contentment that you'll wonder why you didn't start sooner. Remember: everything you've ever done or will ever do—your past, present, and future—is all for you. Own it.

Day 45.

This Is How We Coexist

"Everyone walks their own unseen journey. Wish them peace—and keep walking yours."

Do you get along with people—not just the ones you choose to be around, but the ones who challenge you or rub you the wrong way? Don't answer right away. First, understand this: true coexistence doesn't mean biting your tongue to avoid conflict. It means moving through social interactions—especially the challenging ones—without being derailed by emotion.

Well, do you?

Human connection is a big part of life. While we each walk our own path, we're all part of a bigger picture. That's why it's important to develop the ability to coexist peacefully—without letting others' actions or opinions knock us off balance. One of the best ways to stay unbothered is to understand the reasons behind what we—and they—do.

Think of a tree in a forest. While it grows tall and strong on its own, it's also part of a larger ecosystem. To thrive, it learns to spread its roots through the soil alongside its neighbors, intertwining with other plants until it finds its way to the sky. The tree is unique, living its own life, but it thrives because of the relationships it shares—with the surrounding vegetation, the soil, the rain, the animals, and even the air. Its journey is solitary, but it is deeply connected to something much bigger.

Similarly, everyone you encounter is on their own journey. They have a purpose, and they're acting in pursuit of the person they are becoming. Maybe their journey is to understand life, grow as a parent, experience love, learn independence through isolation, or overcome fear or loss. The possibilities are endless, each one as unique as the individual. Our paths rarely start and end in the same place. We don't look the same, act the same, or think the same, and for most of us, we don't end up where we began.

Like the tree in the forest, our metamorphosis spans a lifetime. There will be times when we're having a bad day and take it out on someone else—or when someone else does the same to us. But this is part of our journey, shaped by the lessons and circumstances we're working through in any given moment.

So, remember this: wherever someone is on their journey, that's exactly where they're meant to be. If they say something offensive, seem out of sorts, or act in a way that bothers you, don't feel the need to understand it. They are simply doing what feels right to them in that moment. If someone gets under your skin, it's not because you've done something wrong. You've just crossed paths while their life happens to be on rough terrain.

Let that sink in. Spend some time with it. We don't need to understand everything others do, but we can find peace in knowing that it makes sense to them.

If it hadn't been you, it likely would've been someone else—because what they're reacting to isn't personal. It's part of their process. Recognizing this requires emotional maturity, but when you embrace it, this wisdom becomes the foundation for living undisturbed by others. It's what allows us to love our neighbors—and even complete strangers. It's what lets us smile when insulted and embrace loved ones, even when their words are hurtful or reckless. It's what allows us all to coexist.

Note: This does not excuse anyone's actions, nor does it suggest that people are not responsible for their behavior. It's simply an effort to explain why some things unfold the way they do. Of course, there are individuals whose path includes violence, anger, or control—and it's important to keep your distance from such people. We can recognize that they, too, are on a journey and hope they find a swift path to self-love—while choosing not to become entangled in their life lessons. Again, this is not about excusing anyone—it's about understanding everyone.

When we realize that each of us is having an individual experience that contributes to a collective one, we open ourselves to seeing the world in a new way—a way that makes peaceful coexistence possible. Remember: We're all on our own journeys. Let go of the need to fix, change, or fully understand others, and instead, embrace the idea that everyone is doing their best to reach their destination—just as you are. Truly grasping this is how we live in harmony with everyone and navigate life unbothered by anyone—this is how we coexist.

Just imagine how different life could feel if you released the emotional weight of reacting to others—if you could simply coexist, calm, grounded, and at peace.

The answer: It feels free.

And once you taste that freedom, you'll understand why it was worth the wait.

Day 46.

Faith

"When life tests your spirit, it is faith that will carry you home—guiding you back to yourself and the life you were always meant to live."

You've probably heard the saying, "like water off a duck's back"—the art of moving through life without letting anything weigh you down. It's a simple image, but a powerful one: the water glides off the duck's feathers, never soaking in, never slowing it down. Ducks are able to do what they love— swim and be free—because of a special wax-like coating on their feathers. They have oil glands at the base of their tails, which create a natural, water-resistant barrier. Thanks to this natural protection, cold water simply rolls off—leaving them free to enjoy their day, undisturbed.

Like ducks, we also have a protective layer that keeps us afloat and safe. But ours isn't on the outside—it's within us, and it's called faith. Faith is a deep, unwavering belief—an inner knowing—that stays firm in the face of outside forces. It's a conviction so powerful that it becomes a personal law, one that remains steadfast, even after the spirit of the individual is tested. Faith keeps us grounded, even through our greatest challenges. No matter what happens around you, faith will endure.

As you progress on your journey, it's inevitable that your convictions will be tested—that your faith will be called upon. Faith is what will drive you forward. Remember, if you've made it this far, you're already building a strong foundation of faith. Strengthen this foundation through personal growth, healing, gratitude, and generosity, and use it as support during times of doubt. When life presents obstacles or setbacks, faith becomes your anchor. It might not always be easy, but it's in those moments that your belief in yourself can propel you forward, guiding you toward your purpose.

For years I woke every day feeling like my life had spiraled so far down the wrong road that I would never find my way back. I had worked around the clock, day in and day out, because I believed I had no choice. Then one day, the very thing I needed to keep going was suddenly failing: my health. The relationships I had once cherished were now fractured, with friends and family falling into three categories—the absent, the abusive, and the broken.

But somehow, through the smoke and haze, I saw the faces of my children. I felt the warmth of my grandparents' love. And, deep inside, I remembered the faith of the small boy I once was—the boy who loved going to church, who believed that something greater was watching over him, that he was never alone. In those moments of reflection, I was guided back to myself. It was my faith that carried me home.

Yours may be different. Faith doesn't have to be tied to religious belief; it can take many forms—trust in yourself, confidence in those around you, or a quiet knowing that your journey has meaning, even if it's not yet clear. It's not about a particular doctrine or worldview, but about believing that you have what it takes to move forward, even when the way seems uncertain.

Here's something important to remember: Faith isn't just belief—it's a muscle. One that needs practice, attention, and care to stay strong. We must work on our faith—feed it, nurture it, and strengthen it—so it can support us when we need it most. The more you reinforce it with small daily practices—affirmations, conscious choices, or simply trusting yourself—the stronger your faith will grow. Every time you act with integrity, every time you choose self-love over doubt, you're reinforcing that protective layer within, becoming a stronger version of yourself.

The strength of your faith is what keeps you grounded through life's uncertainty. Like water rolling off a duck's back, your faith shields you from external influences that might derail your journey to becoming your true self. As you continue working toward the new you, your faith will naturally grow stronger. Remember, acting with integrity and self-love will serve you best. It's not just about how we grow mentally, but also how we carry ourselves in the world that shapes the best version of who we are.

Never forget that you are the architect of your own journey. Regularly remind yourself of your goals, the reasons behind them, and why they matter. When challenges arise, your faith will lead you exactly where you're meant to be.

Day 47.

World Peace

"When we take responsibility for how we show up in the world, we move closer to creating a peaceful world for everyone."

Imagine leaving your home for a trip to the grocery store. This time, everything feels different—people are kind to one another. From the moment you step outside, to your drive, and even inside the store, you're surrounded by joy, peace, and excitement. In the store, there's harmony—people exchange pleasantries in the aisles, smiling and saying hello. A friendly stranger invites you to go ahead of them at checkout, and you share a lovely conversation with the cashier. This is what it looks like when everyone acts from a place of kindness. It's called peace—and when enough people live this way, it can grow into "world peace." It may feel like a distant dream, but the truth is: it starts at home—one person at a time.

Wouldn't world peace be wonderful? I think we can all agree on that. How often do pop songs and pageant contestants express their wishes for world peace? Many of us can probably hear John Lennon's voice urging us to "Give peace a chance." But why haven't we achieved it yet? In short, we weren't quite ready—but it feels like we're beginning to be.

World peace isn't something that can be decided by a vote or by an organization. It's not as simple as declaring, "Alright, everyone, let's stop disagreeing. From this point forward, we'll all be at peace." That's not how it works. Instead, world peace is a mindset—an understanding that begins on an individual level. The key word here is "individual." It starts when one person chooses to live in a state of universal coexistence and goodwill, and makes changes in their life to match this decision. When enough people adopt this mindset, creating a noticeable shift, you begin to see masses of individuals working toward a common goal. This is the beginning of world peace: a cumulative effort where each person takes steps toward their own personal growth.

What does this "personal growth" look like? It's the growth that comes from realizing we each have the power to create our own reality—and that peace is possible without suffering. It's a life of coexisting with others, where individuals walk their own journeys in harmony with the journeys of those around them. It's about taking responsibility for how we show up in the world, every moment of every day. The shift from reacting with anger, fear, or frustration to responding with calm and compassion doesn't have to happen in big moments. In fact, it starts in the smallest of moments—like choosing not to snap at someone who cuts you off in traffic.

This vision of peace, while ideal, shows us what's possible when we all embody kindness and understanding. It doesn't mean we live in a perfect world, but it does mean that we are actively working toward creating a better, more peaceful reality every time we choose peace over conflict. It's easy to see how such a world might feel distant, but the journey toward it begins with each of us changing how we approach our own lives.

So, how do you know if you're on the right path? A common question that comes up is, "How will I know when I've taken steps toward peace?" The answer is simple: If you're reading this of your own free will, driven by a desire to improve your life, then you've already begun. When you awaken to the fact that joy is possible in every moment, living peacefully is no longer an option—it becomes a natural byproduct of life, because there's no other way to live.

By now, you know you're on a path to personal freedom. You've seen there's more to life than the "rat race," and that emotions like anger, fear, doubt, shame, envy, and stress are optional—they are states we can choose, or choose not, to live in. This journey, this awakening to the reality that a higher state of awareness is both possible and attainable, is what makes world peace possible.

As you continue, you'll notice shifts in your interactions, thoughts, and environment. Small acts of kindness, a peaceful attitude, and a deeper connection to others will all become part of your everyday life. This personal transformation doesn't just benefit you—it ripples outward, influencing those around you. This is how world peace begins: one person at a time.

So go ahead—take a moment to appreciate how far you've come. There's greatness waiting for all of us as we realize the endless possibilities ahead. We each arrive at this point in our own time, and wherever you are on your journey, know that you're exactly where you're meant to be. Be proud and excited—because this is what peace feels like. As you continue your journey, remember: you're not only shaping your own world, but also helping create a more peaceful world for everyone—and that's worth celebrating!

Day 48.

Teach

Teaching is one of the most powerful ways to learn. While it's often described as a gift we give to others, one of its greatest blessings is how it deepens our own understanding. Sometimes, the best way to truly grasp something is to teach it.

Have you ever taught someone a skill—like changing a tire or baking a cake? Teaching is more than simply showing someone how it's done—it's more than just "teaching them how to fish." Teaching is a process that begins long before a student ever appears. To teach something, to pass knowledge along to someone else, you must first master it yourself. You might be able to describe the action of tying a shoe, but to break it down clearly so someone else can do it, you need to understand it fully—you need to master it.

I grew up surrounded by educators—teaching was woven into my family's story: my grandfather, my sister, my aunts and uncles, and many of my cousins were teachers. Teaching became part of my own story as well. When I was young, a mentor told me something that has become a truth I hold dear: *"The best way to learn something is to teach it."* That's why, for those of us called to teach (in whatever form that takes), stepping into the role of teacher can be one of the most powerful ways to deepen our own understanding.

Teaching is also a spiritual practice. It's the act of giving back what was given to you. When done with intention, teaching becomes an art of gratitude and a passion for humanity. Passing knowledge to others is more than just sharing information—it becomes a vital step in your own journey. While teaching isn't a requirement, it can deepen your understanding of what you're pursuing and solidify the wisdom you already possess. Many of us reach a point where teaching feels like the next natural step, and if that call comes, we owe it to ourselves to take it seriously.

How do you know if you're called to be a teacher? That's a question only you can answer. The best advice I can offer is to simply allow. Allow the teacher within you to emerge when it's ready—if it chooses to. There's a saying: "When the student is ready, the teacher will appear." When the time comes for a teacher to help you deepen your understanding—like finding this book—one will arrive. I've found this to be true, and many others have as well.

I've also found the opposite to be true: "When the teacher is ready, the student will appear." In other words, the teacher is also on a journey, and when the time comes, the student will arrive. This might take the form of others asking questions, a new job, new friends, or, for me, it took the form of a new book.

As you continue on your journey, stay open and alert to the call to teach. It may come soon, or it may take years. It may never come at all. But living with the awareness that teaching is a possibility will help you stay receptive to new opportunities that open up in your life.

As with all things, don't rush the process. Allow it to unfold and serve you, as every experience does. In the meantime, continue to learn, grow, and practice. Remember, you were once the eager student. When the time comes for you to share what you've learned, it will be your opportunity to guide. It's a beautiful cycle—teaching and learning nourish each other, and in the end, it's the journey itself that shapes us.

One day, without effort or force, you'll teach, your student will learn—and both of you will be changed forever.

Day 49.

Slow Down

"Slow down—not because you're falling behind, but because it's the fastest way to find yourself."

Do you ever slow down?

Do you ever stop to smell the roses, as they say?

Do you see the roses?

Or do you spend your days on autopilot, moving through life without really noticing where you're going?

Think to yourself:

When.

Was.

The.

Last.

Time.

I.

Slowed.

Down?

See what just happened? You slowed down to read this —and it made you think. You noticed how the words were spaced apart. Each word is part of a sentence—but standing alone, it changed the rhythm. It made you pause and reflect.

How often do you do that?

When you're on autopilot—whatever that looks like for you—who or what is steering your thoughts, words, and actions? Is it your rational mind—the part of you that slows down, reflects, and chooses with intention? Or do you sometimes find yourself acting without thinking, just hoping for the best? What if, instead of rushing through everything, you gave yourself space—to absorb, to reflect, to think more clearly? What if you slowed down?

What if you took a step back? Imagine if every thought, word, and action were intentional—made to improve your life.

It's possible—and even likely—when you slow down and give yourself time to think. Just ask yourself:

- What's happening right now?

- What are my possibilities?

- What are my options?

- How will these thoughts or actions affect my life?

- What can I learn from this experience?

These are just a few questions to help you pause and reflect. Everything you've learned on your journey so far can guide you—especially if you make it a point to apply that knowledge every day.

Now that you have a roadmap for where you want to go, and a vision of the person you want to become, you always have the option to slow down. By doing so, you ensure you're taking the necessary steps to get there.

Make room for the new you to emerge. It's a simple three-step process:

1.   **Decide** who you want to become.

2.   **Learn** how to become that person.

3.   **Put what you know into practice**—until it becomes who you are.

Step three is where everything comes together—you begin to embody the wise individual you've always been.

Slow.

Down.

At this point, you've spent time learning how to navigate your journey. You've defined the path—now it's time to turn your hard work into tangible results. And the key to doing this is slowing down.

Slowing down offers more than peace of mind—it gives you control. Just a few of the benefits:

- You have time to choose actions that align with your goals.

- You spot setbacks and pitfalls before they happen.

- You practice gratitude more easily.

- You stay calm and collected.

- You maintain the mindset you choose.

Ironically, slowing down is often the fastest way to get where you want to go.

So, with all this in mind, what will you do next?

Stop—don't answer right away. Take a moment to think about it.

Now—do it.

Day 50.

Shine

"Be yourself, boldly and brightly, for your true light is the greatest gift you can give to the world. And in the end, authenticity is the only way to live."

Let your light shine—and let it shine bright.

What does this mean? It means be yourself. Be the truest version of yourself—the one you know deep down and are always becoming. Let the inner you—the one full of love, wisdom, and creativity—be the version that others see in the world.

Your life, your journey, is ever-flowing and steady. Like the figure-eight infinity loop, there is no end—you exist in a state of continual evolution, always changing, always steering the ship from the present.

You've chosen a path of understanding and self-discovery—a path that leads you toward peace, joy, and abundance. Your journey won't always be easy, but it will always continue, and it will be deeply rewarding.

As you move forward, the further you go, the easier it becomes to maintain momentum. Once the door to possibilities is opened to you, you will never forget what you've learned. The drive to evolve, to reach your greatness, will always be your guiding force.

So, what do you do now? There is only the continuation of forward motion and the call to shine. Shine as yourself—as the true you. Shine unapologetically, because being authentic and true to who you are is the ultimate gift you can give yourself. It's the best example you can set for the world and the highest state of living you can achieve. And in the end, it's the only way to live.

This version of yourself is patient, kind, aware, and contributes to the highest good of all. When you live from this place, shine your light, and shine it bright. Doing so will inspire you continuously while encouraging others to do the same.

Revisit the readings in this book whenever you feel called. Returning to them may feel like a refresher—a review at times—but it will remind you of who you wish to become and guide you along your path. The journey of self-discovery is lifelong, and the teachings in these pages are tools to guide your next steps, wherever they lead.

When these tools no longer serve you—or when you feel you've outgrown them—seek wisdom elsewhere. Never stop working on yourself, never stop shining, and never stop becoming.

If you haven't already, you will discover that as you make conscious decisions about how to act, think, and move, you become the architect of your own life journey. This realization often comes suddenly, with great surprise. It sparks a motivation that is difficult to capture with words, presenting itself as a reward you won't soon forget.

Remember, your state of being is not determined by what happens in the world—it's determined by how you react to it. When you control your thoughts and behaviors, every experience becomes exactly what you want it to be.

Congratulations on the work you've done so far—and the work you're just beginning. Go with grace, go with ease, be well, and above all else, be yourself.

And now: Shine.

Afterward

"You did the work. And now—you get to live it."

You made it.

Fifty days of showing up. Fifty days of reflection, intention, and choosing to grow. That's no small thing. You've done something powerful—not just by reading, but by letting these words meet you where you are. You've taken genuine steps toward a better version of yourself, one page at a time.

You may still look like the same person—but you've shifted. There's a calm in your presence now. A steadiness in how you speak, how you move. Others may not be able to put their finger on it, but they'll feel it—something about you is different. You've returned to yourself. Not the self shaped by fear or expectation, but one rooted in clarity, honesty, and truth.

You've built something inside you that won't break—not even when life tests it. You'll draw from this work in unexpected ways: A moment of stillness. A wiser choice. A deeper breath. These shifts stay with you, even long after the final page.

As you move forward, trust yourself. Have faith in what's still unfolding. Let grace walk beside you. Let your growth carry you. And let it reflect back the truth of all you've stepped into.

This journey doesn't end here. You've just completed something powerful—but the work lives on. When you return, you'll see these pages differently—because you'll be seeing them with new eyes.

Maybe you began this book unsure of your next step. Maybe you were caught between who you thought you should be and who you truly are. But by showing up, you've done more than grow—you've remembered.

You've remembered your voice.

You've remembered who's writing this story.

You've remembered what's real.

That's what Personal Mastery really is. It's not something you chase—it's something you uncover. And now, you know where to look.

Keep choosing. Keep listening. Keep writing the next page.

Always remember: who you are is not something you find—it's something you return to. Return as often as you need. There's no wrong time to come home.

With love,
Zach

Final Reflection

This book wasn't written in long stretches of free time. It came together in quiet, late nights—those rare moments when parenting slows just enough for stillness to take hold. It was built page by page, word by word, in the spaces life allowed.

What's here isn't just what I've learned—it's what I've lived. Some days I remembered how to show up with clarity and truth. Other days, I began again. That's the heart of this work: not perfection, but presence.

If something in these pages found its way into your life, I'm grateful. You didn't just read this book—you brought it to life by walking through it.

About the Author

Zachary Fulbright is a writer and coach whose work centers on personal mastery, inner clarity, and spiritual growth. Drawing from his own journey of reflection and transformation, he helps others reconnect with what matters, release what no longer serves them, and live with greater self-awareness and ease.

He believes in the quiet power of change—the kind that doesn't shout, but reshapes you from the inside out. His writing is an invitation to pause, return to yourself, and begin again with intention.

Zachary lives in North Carolina with his two daughters and their English Mastiff, who reminds them all to stay grounded in the present.

Begin again. Any time. Any page.

Let's stay connected.

I offer one-on-one coaching for those walking this path—
quiet, intentional, and rooted in truth.

You can learn more and hear about future writings and
offerings at:
www.ZacharyFulbright.com

www.ingramcontent.com/pod-product-compliance
Lightning Source LLC
Chambersburg PA
CBHW031510120626
46545CB00005B/1821